This Book Belongs to

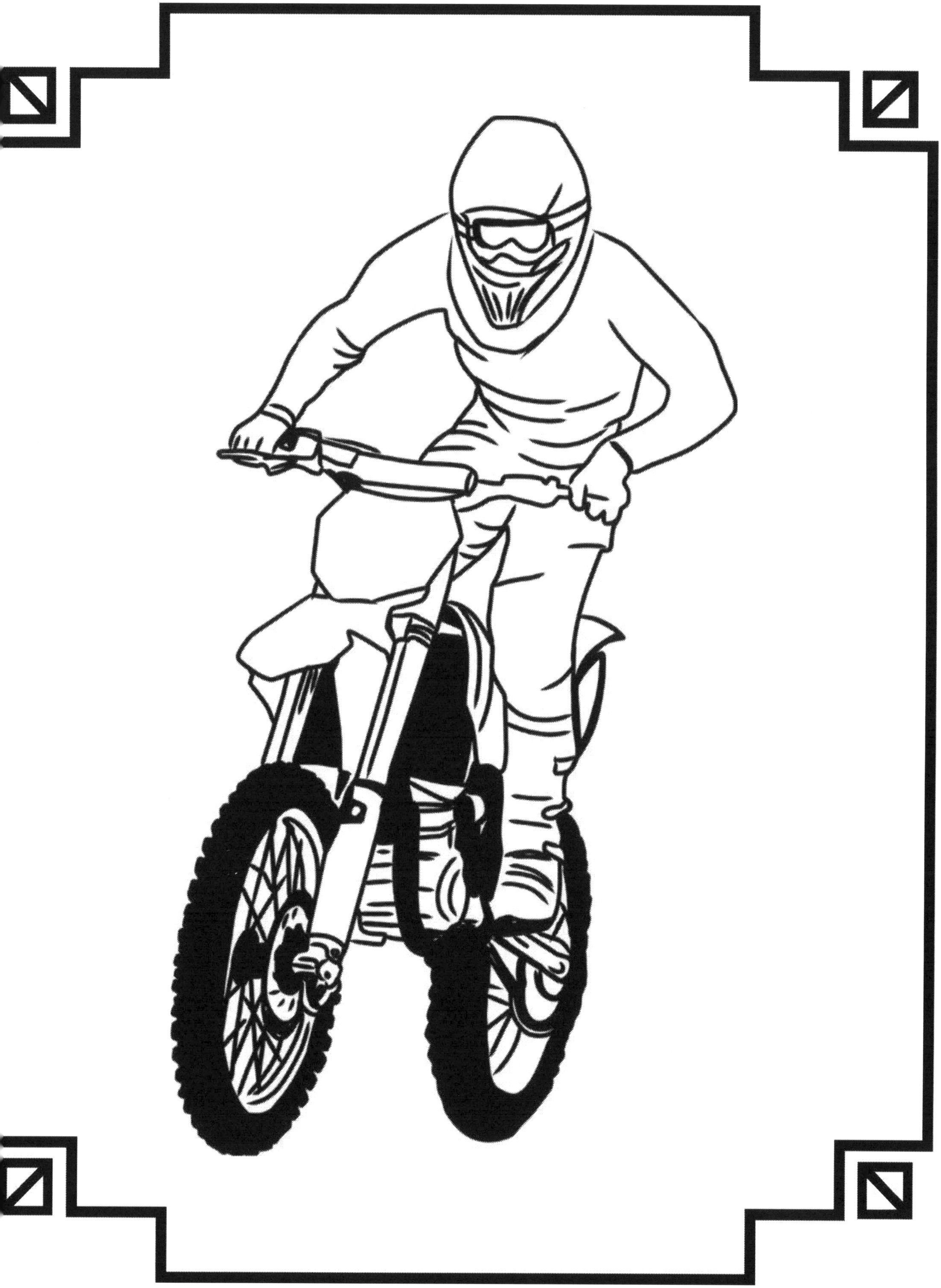

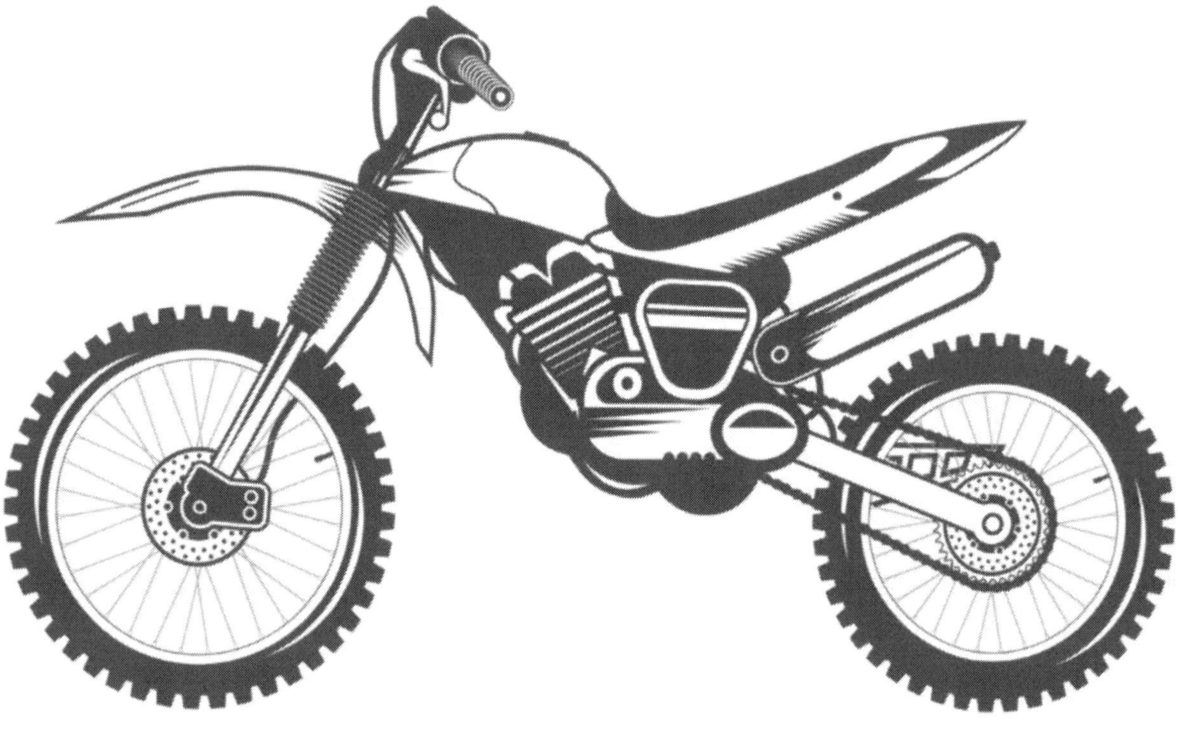

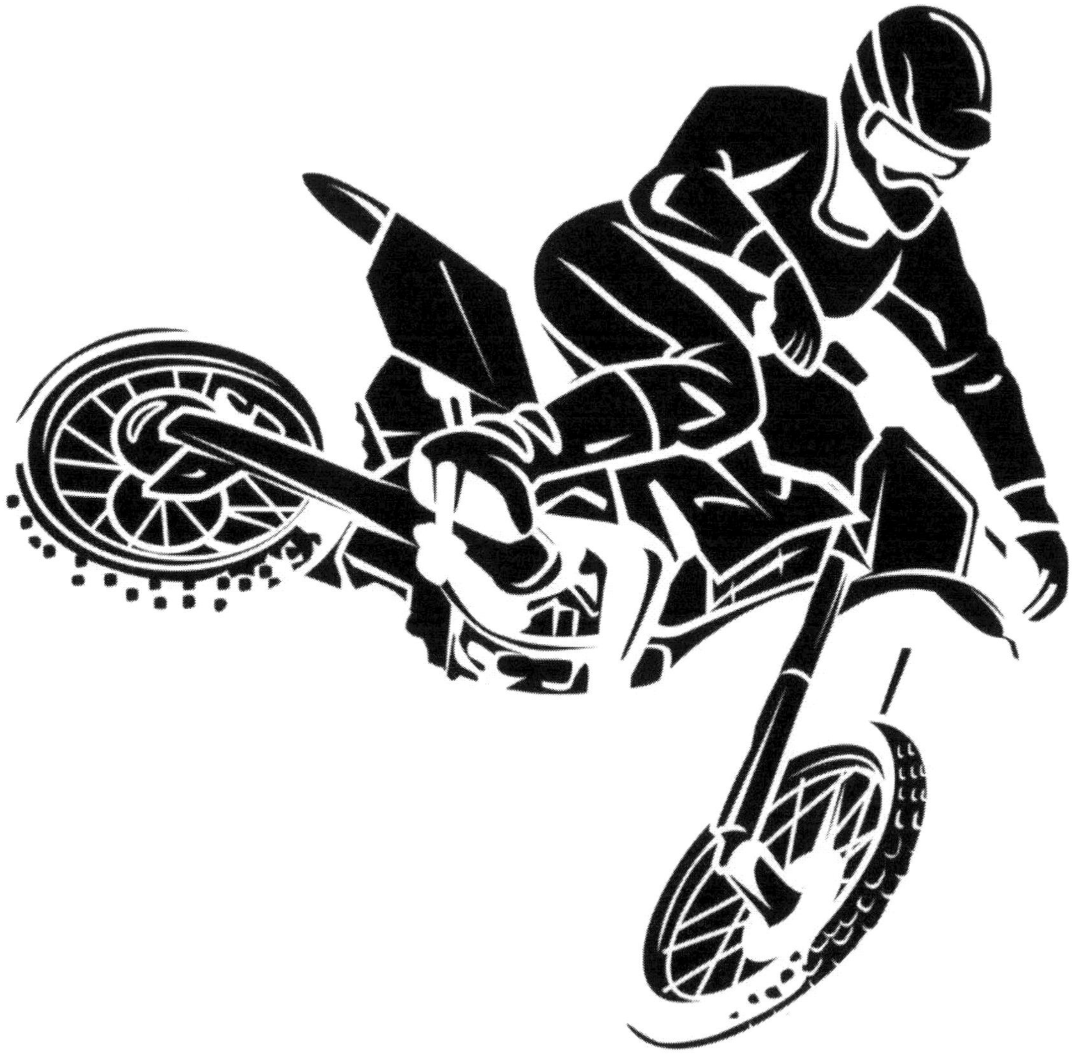

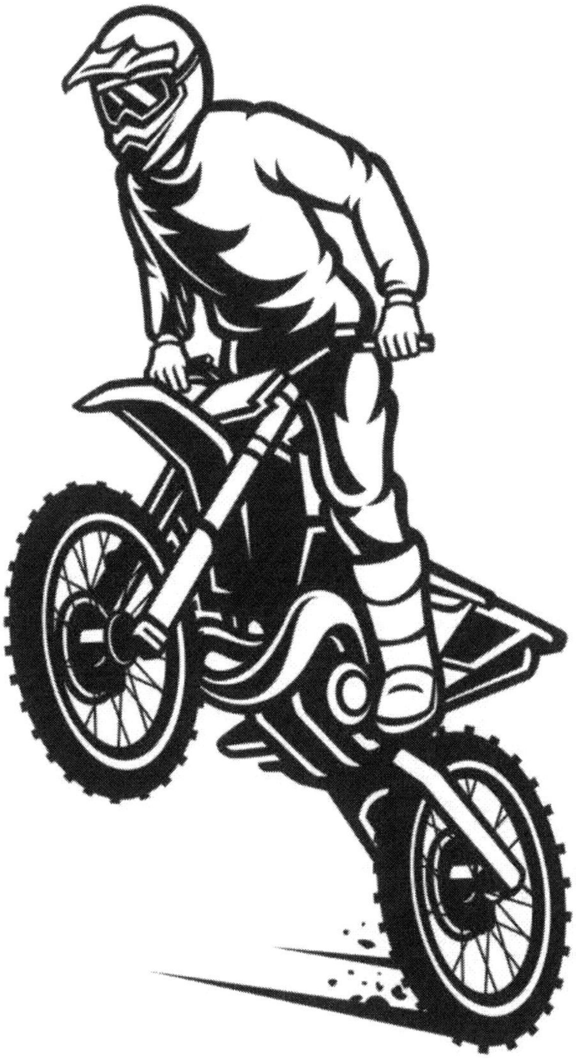

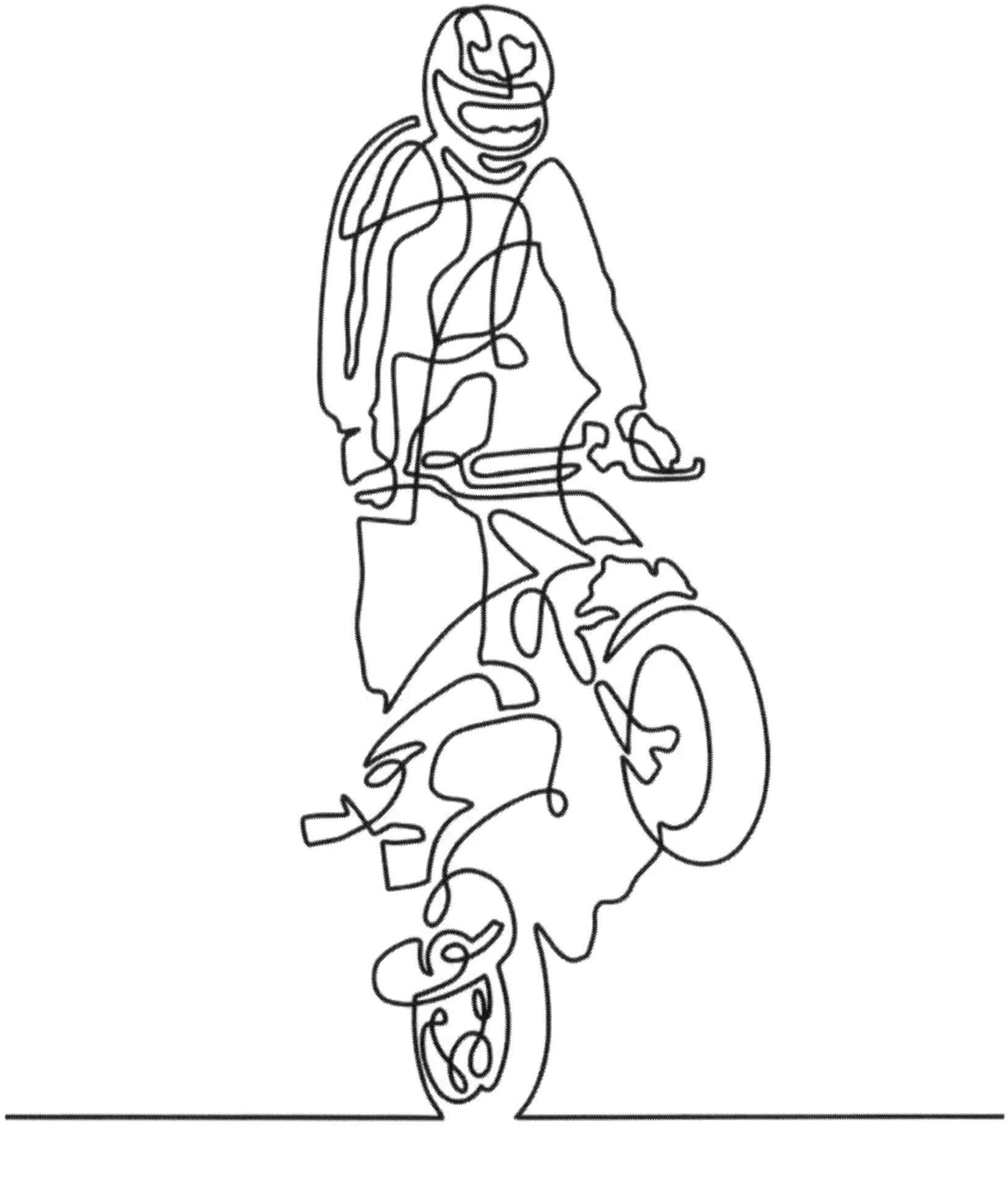

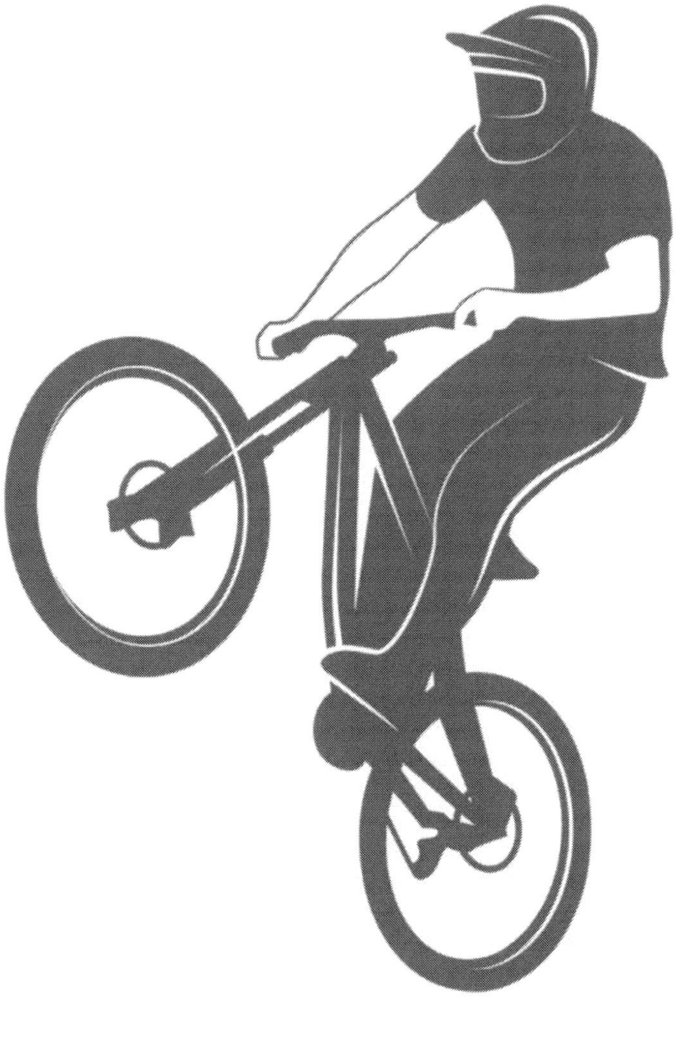

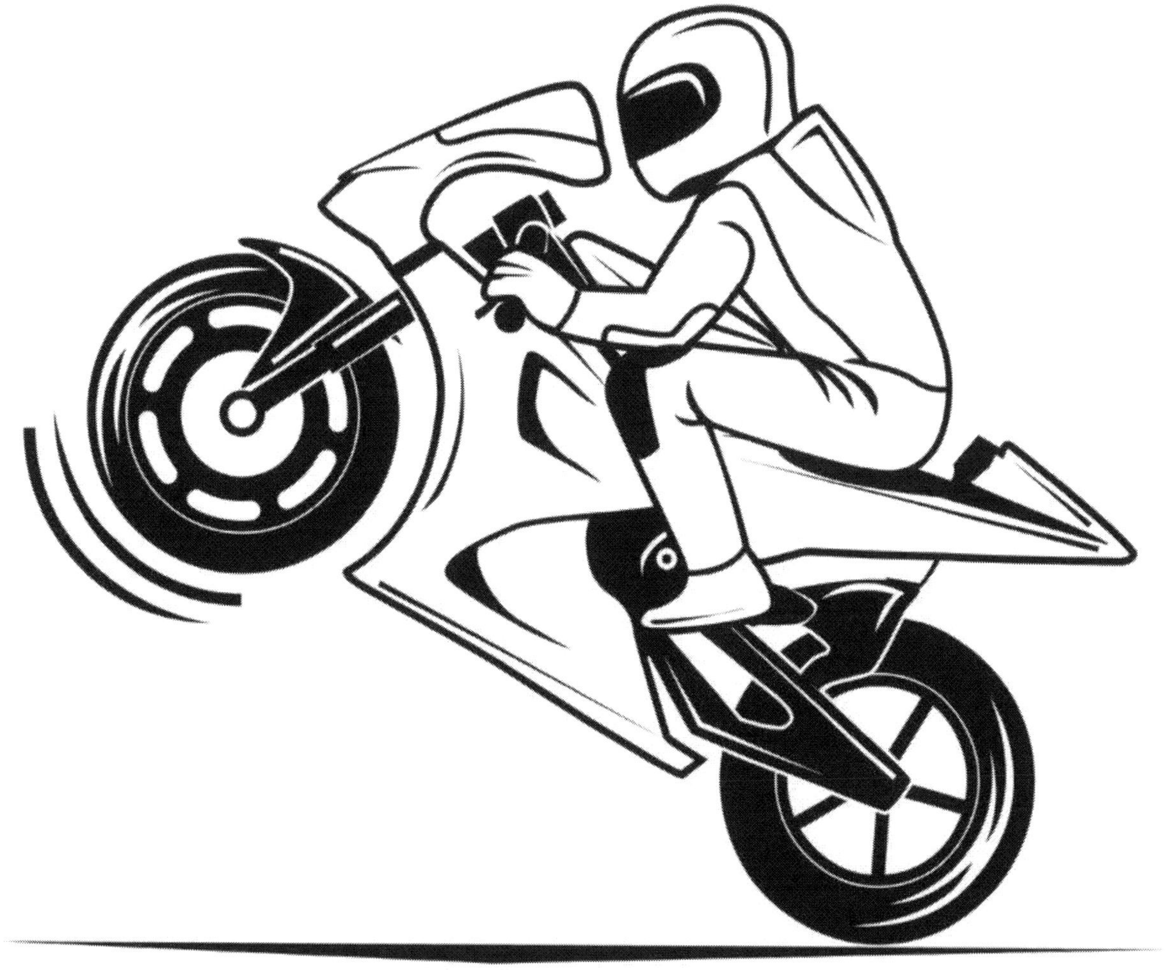

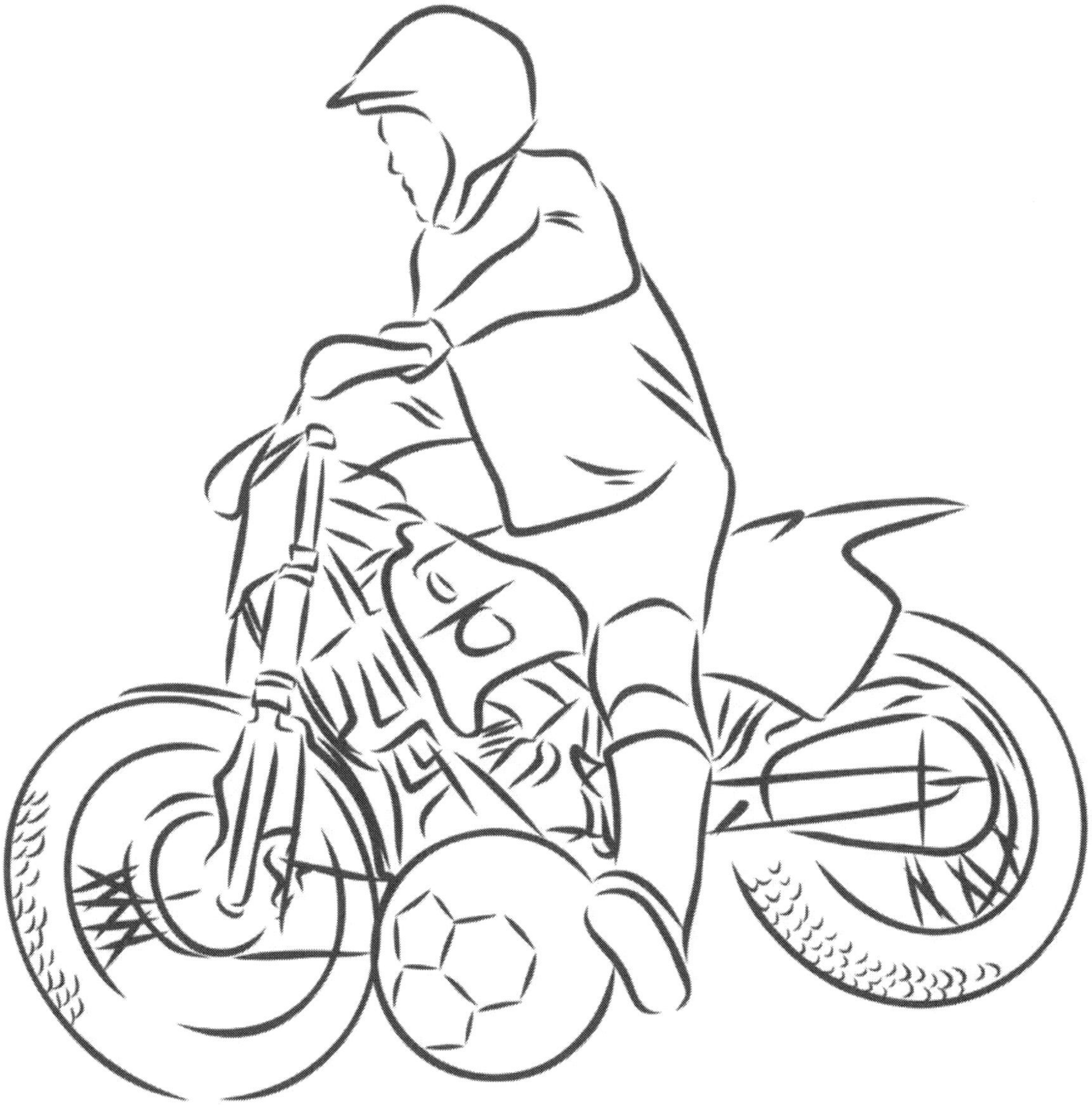

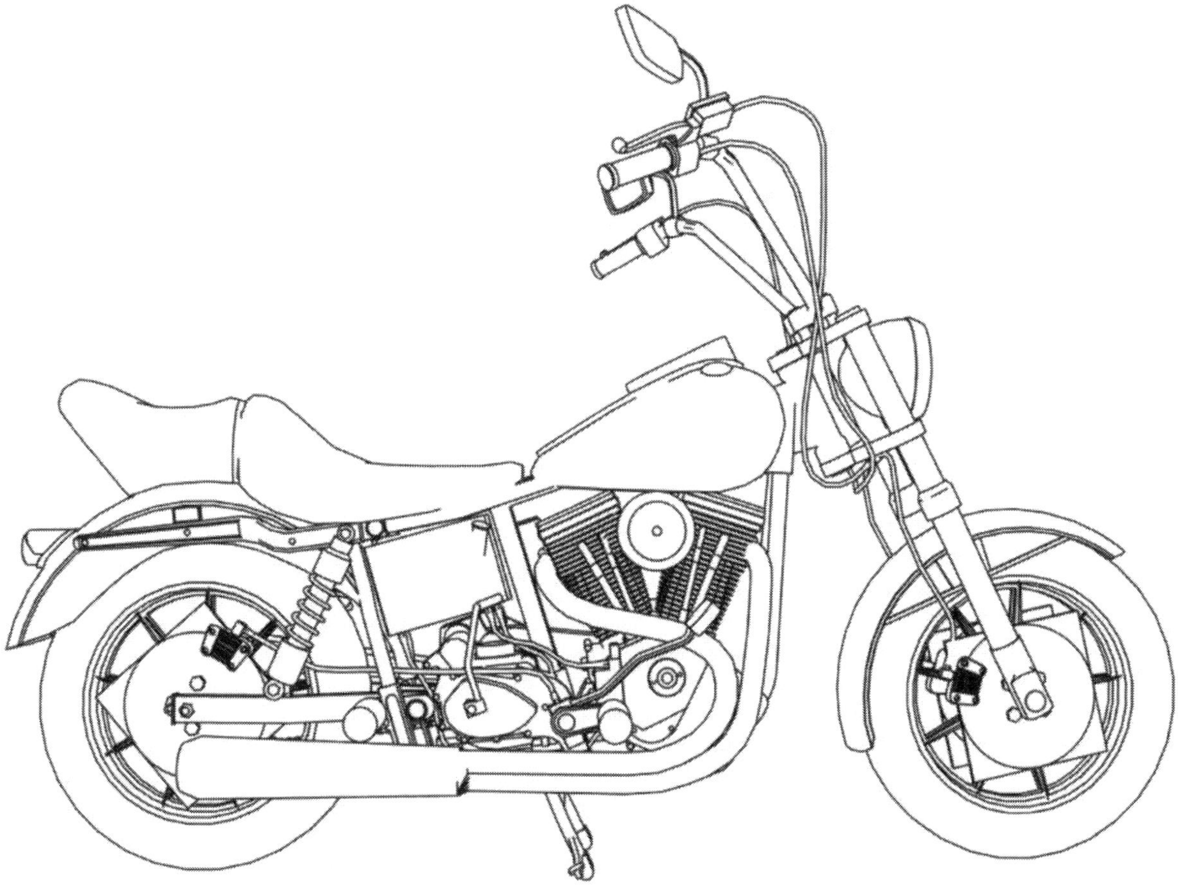

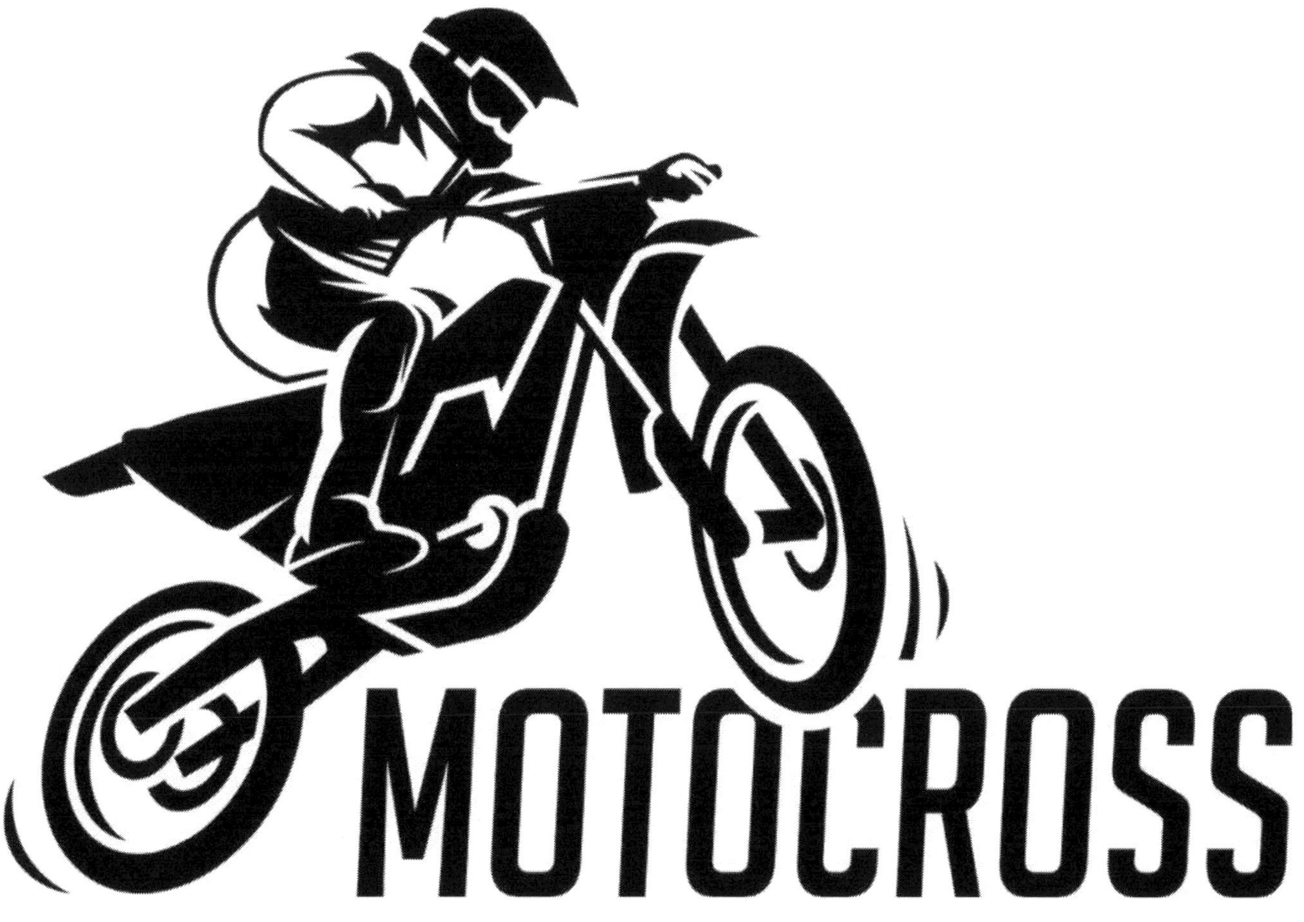
MOTOCROSS

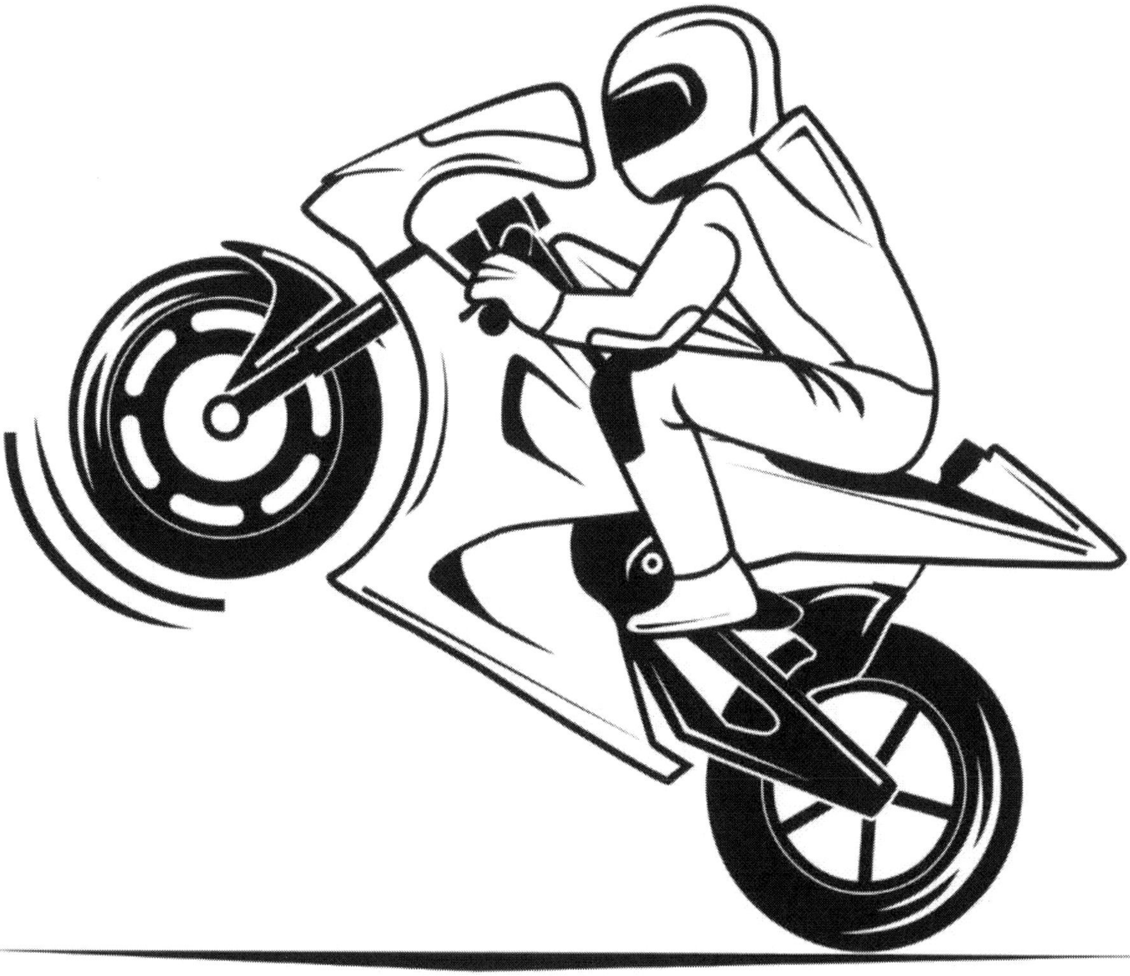

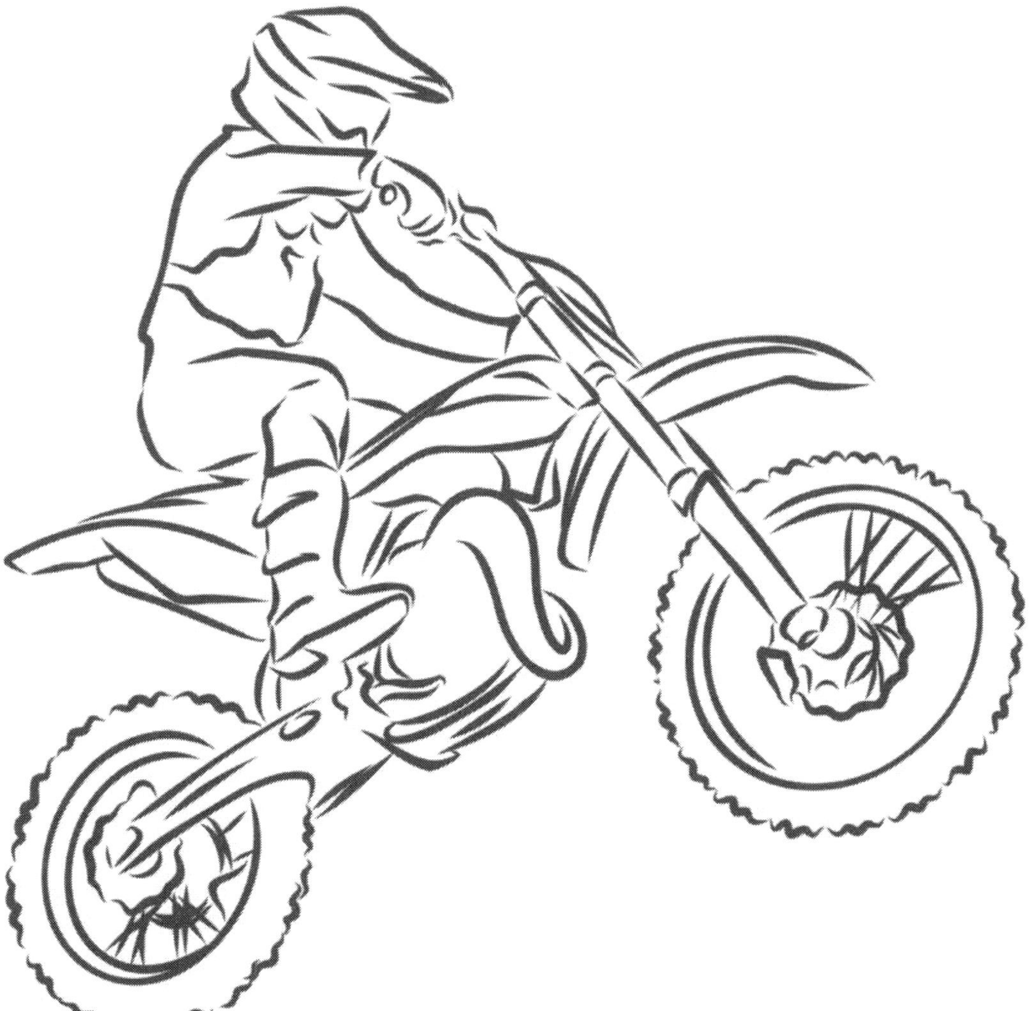

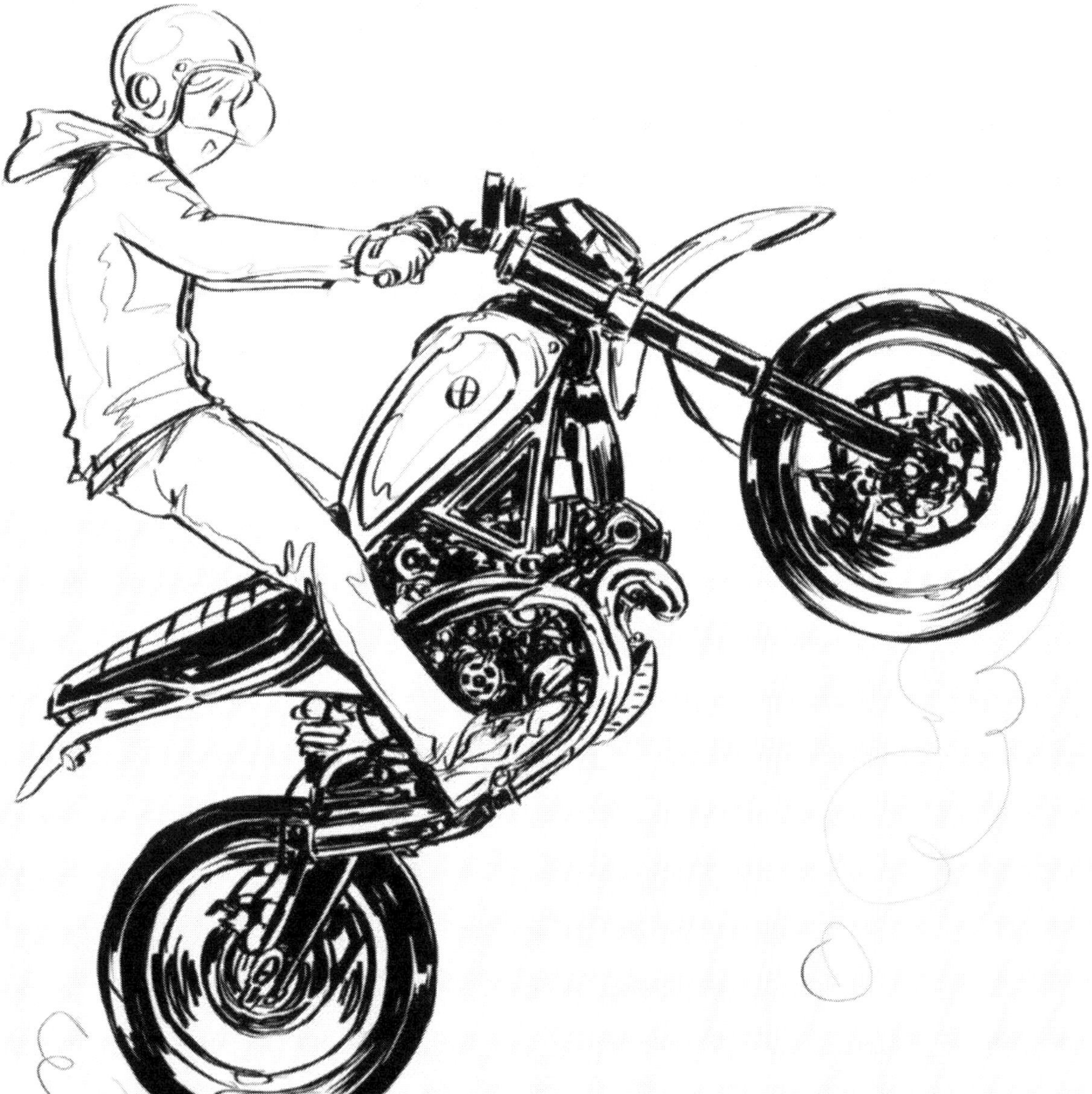

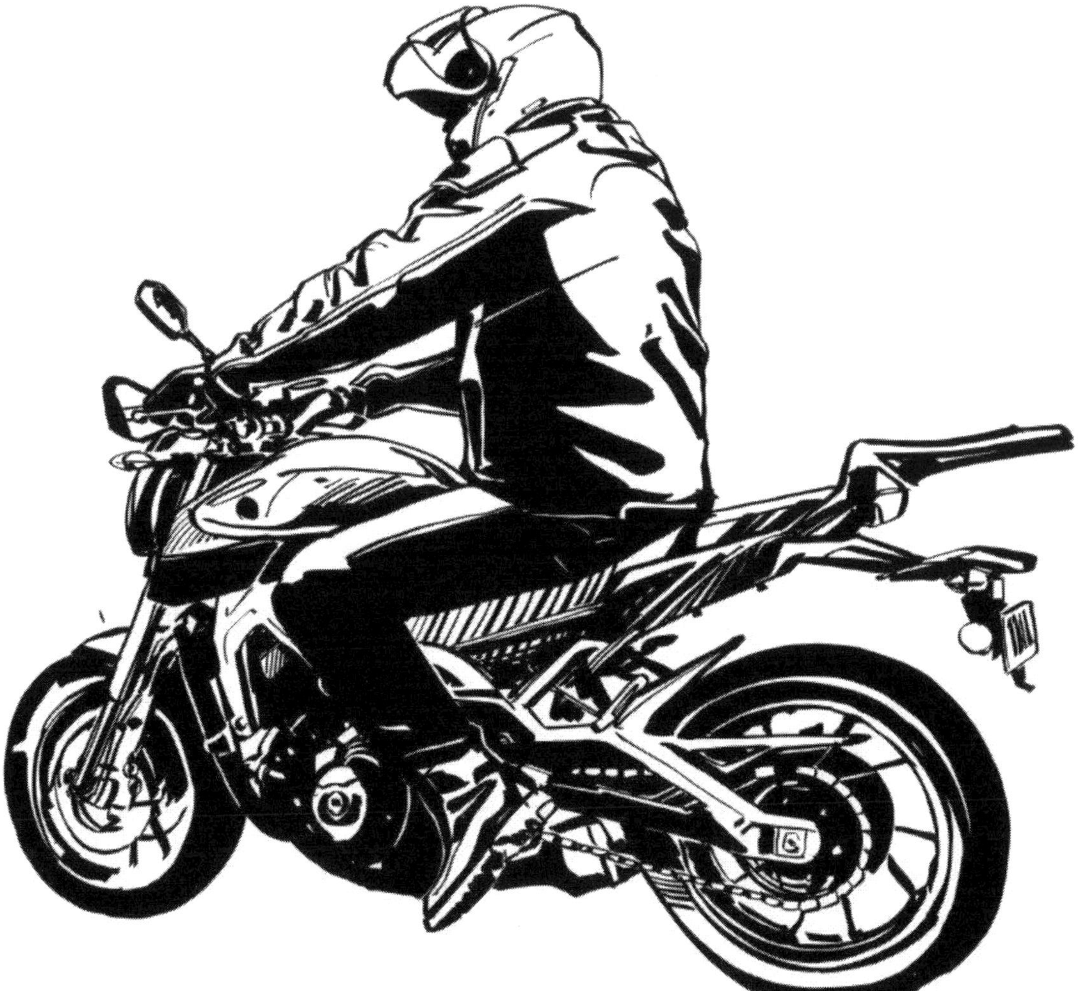

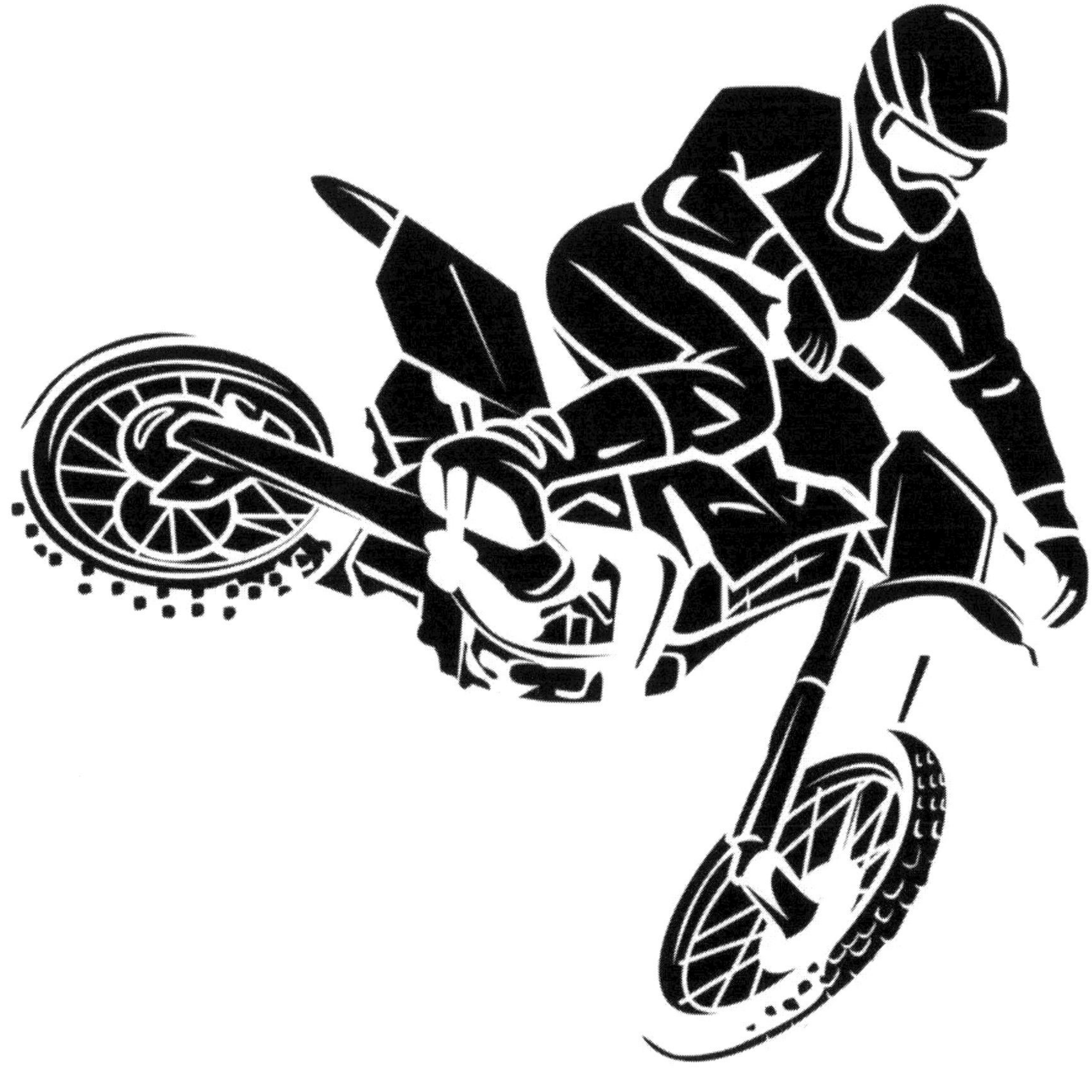

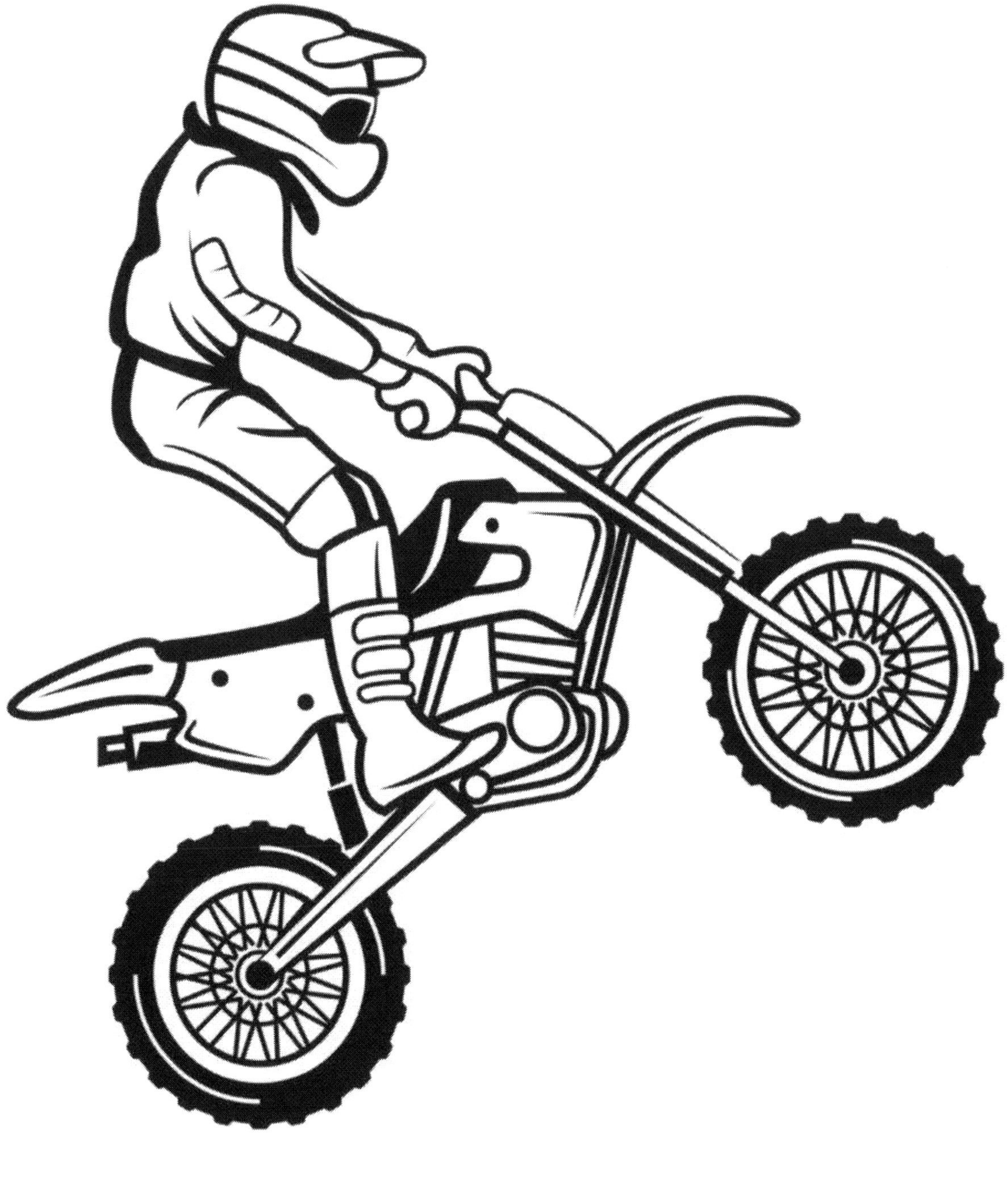

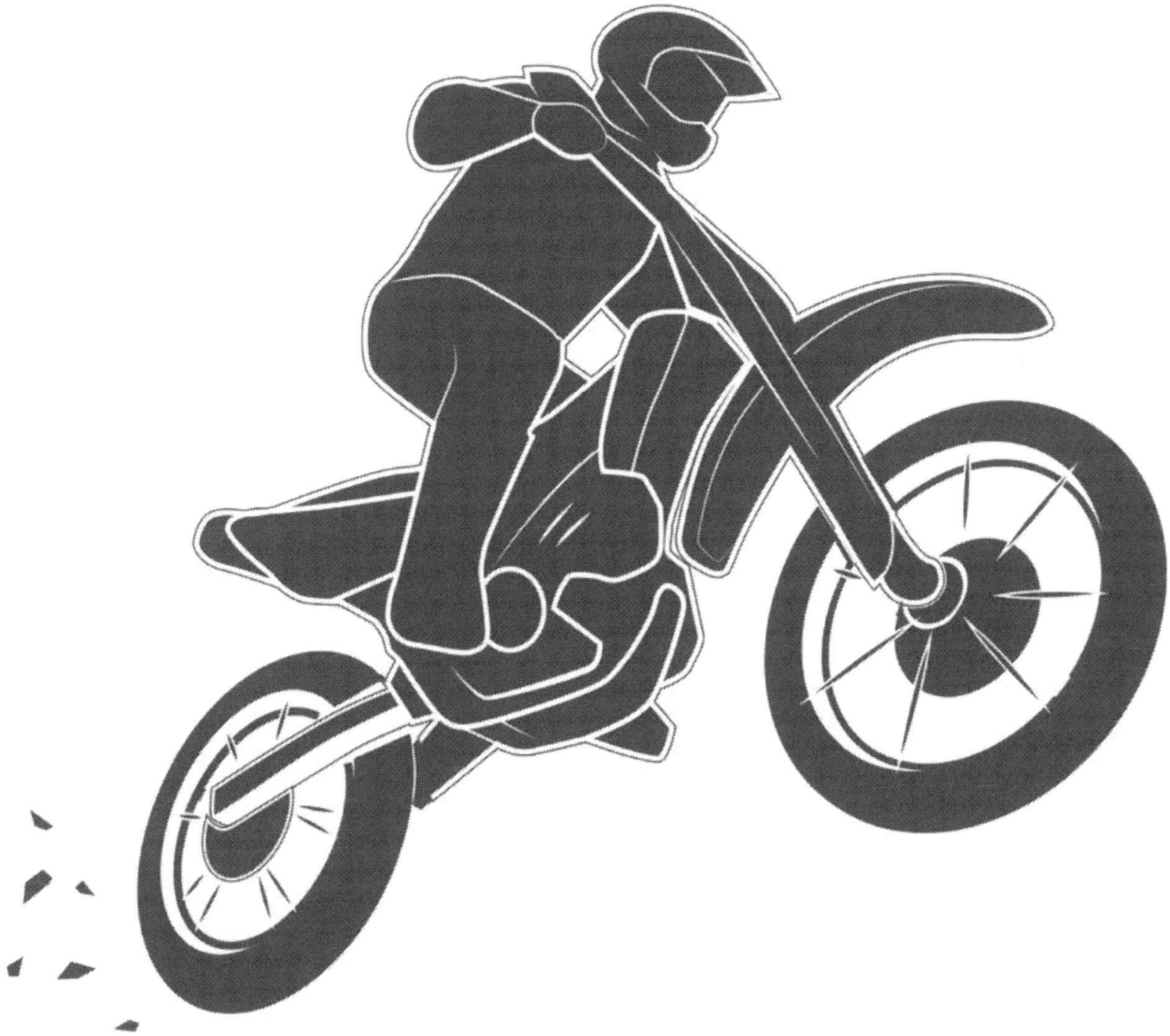

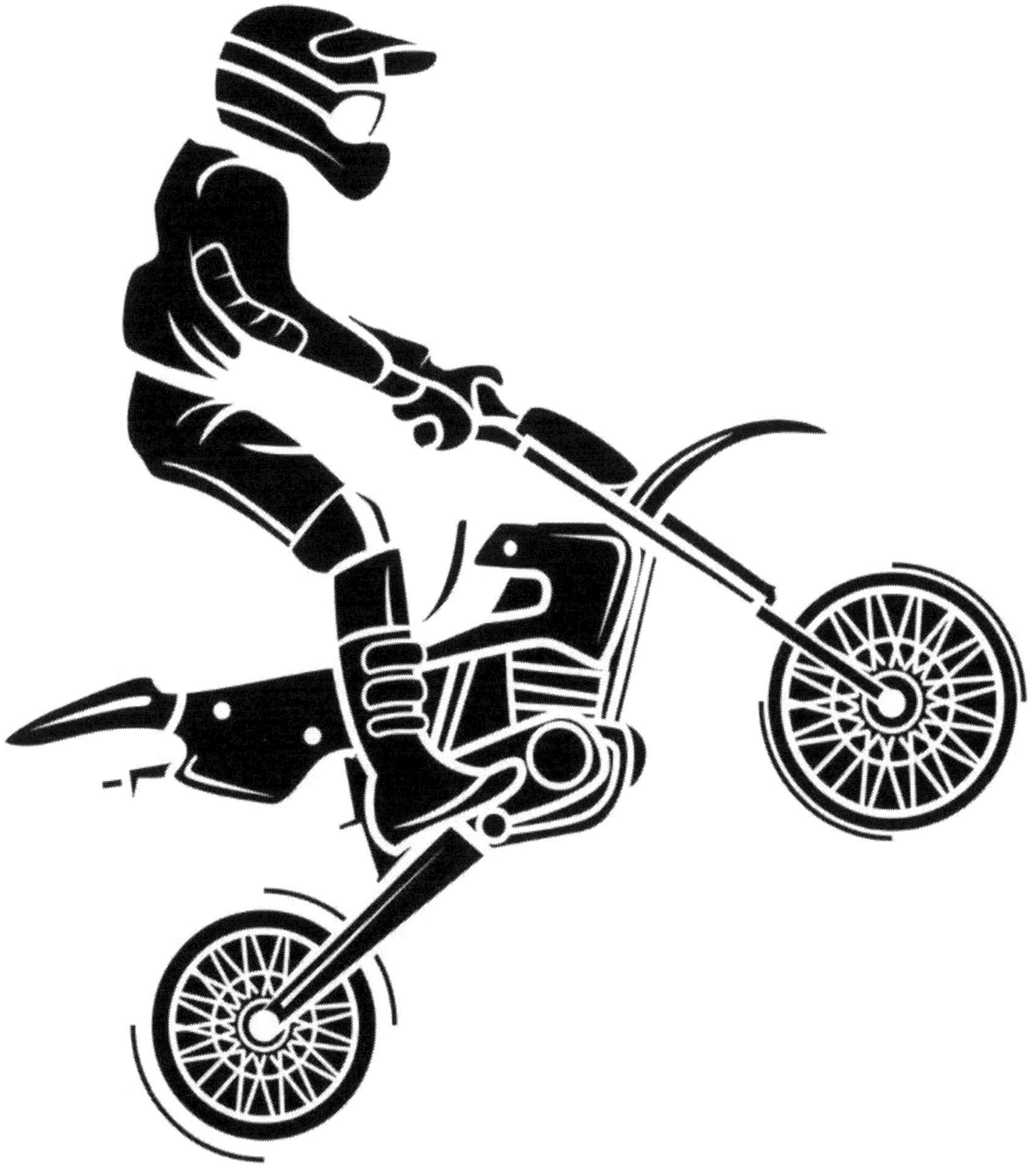

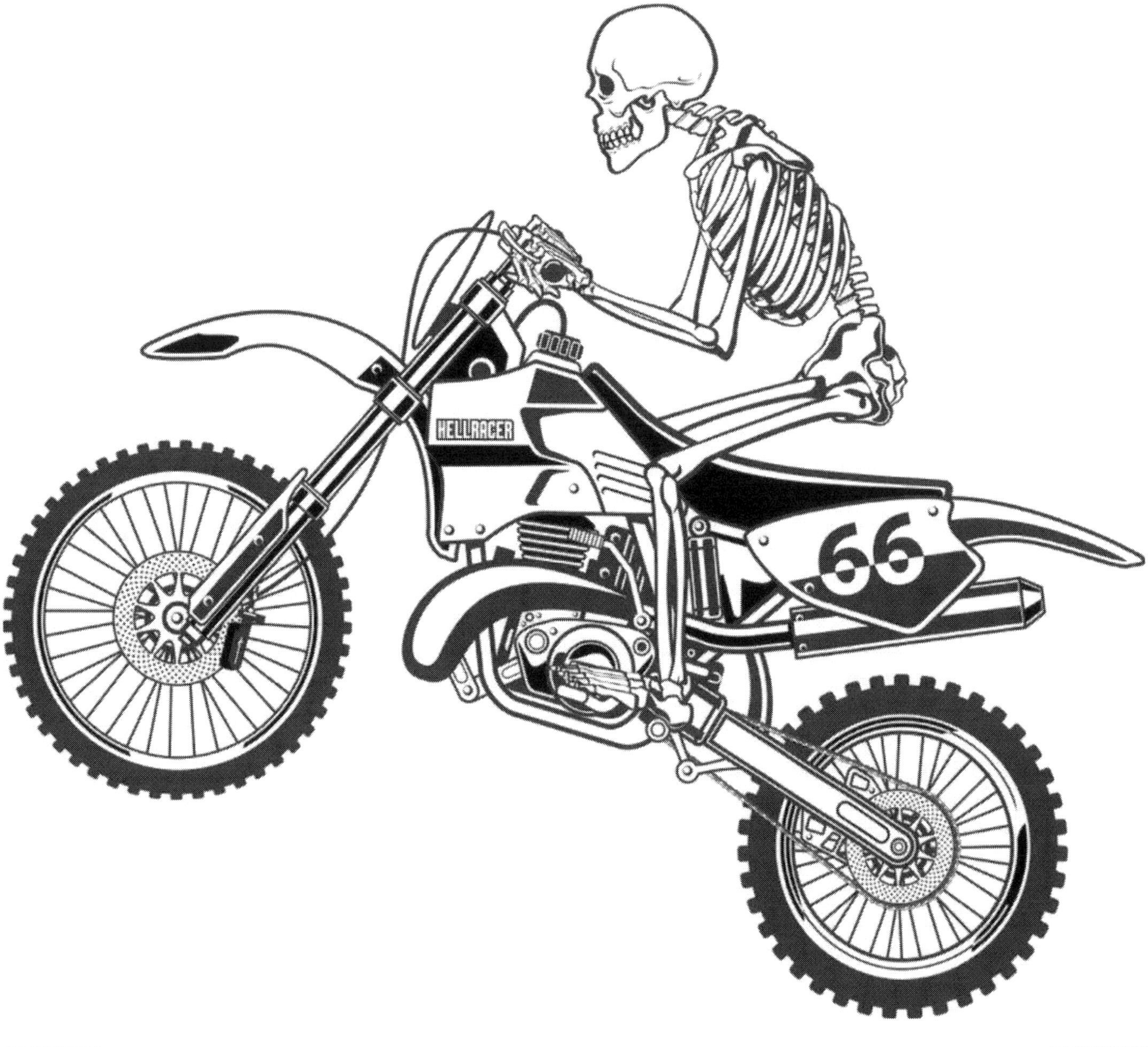
HELLRACER
66

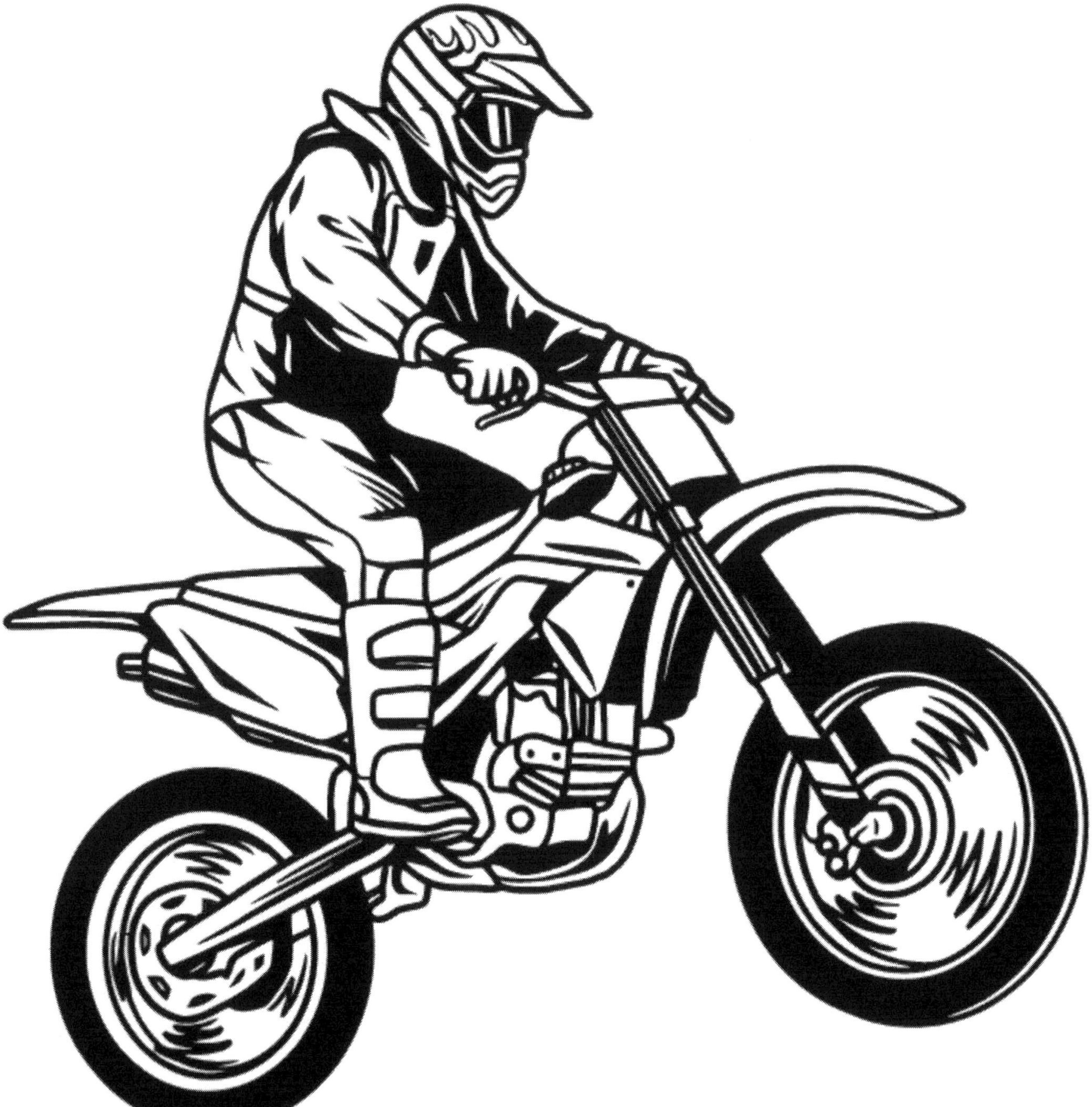

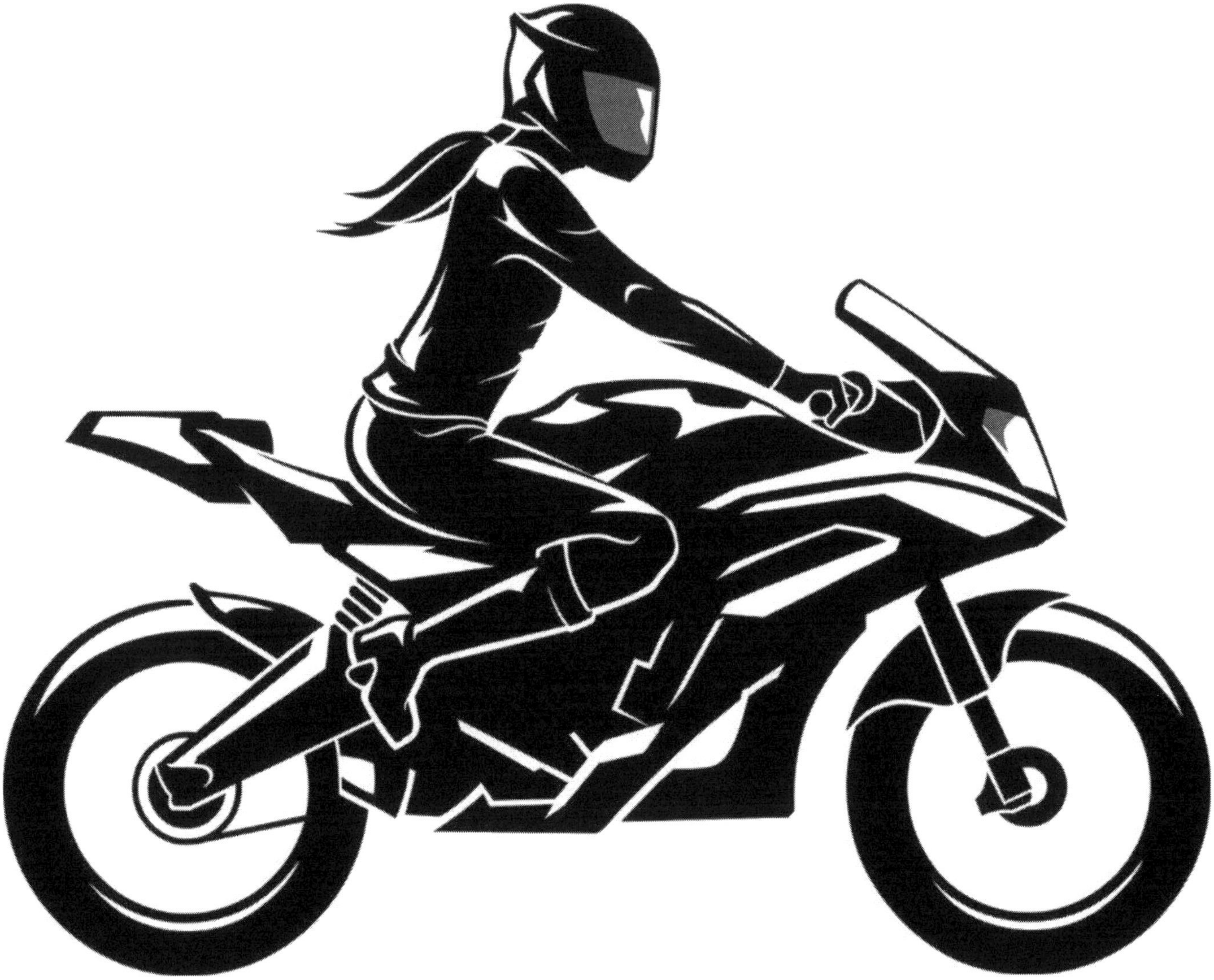

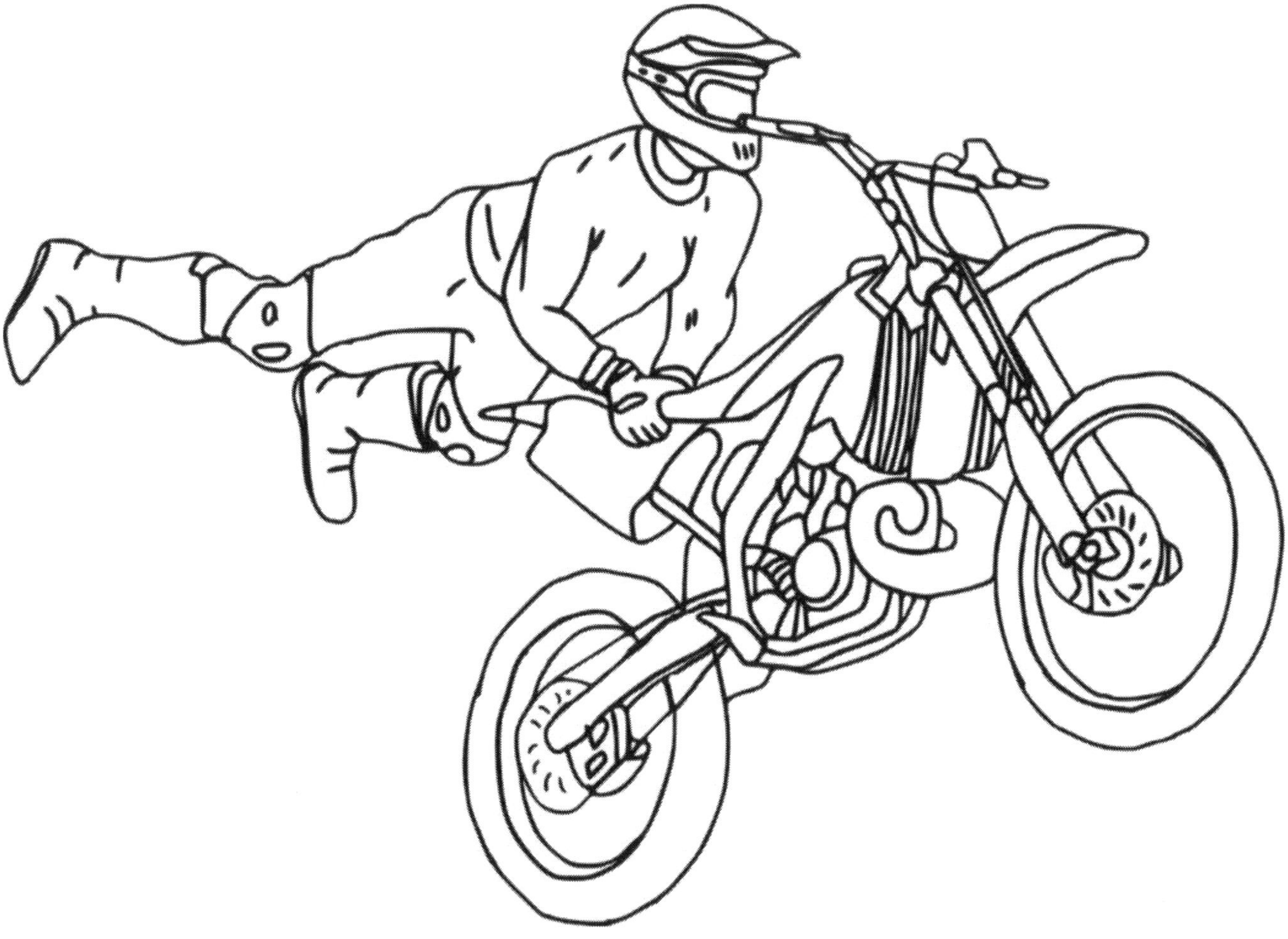

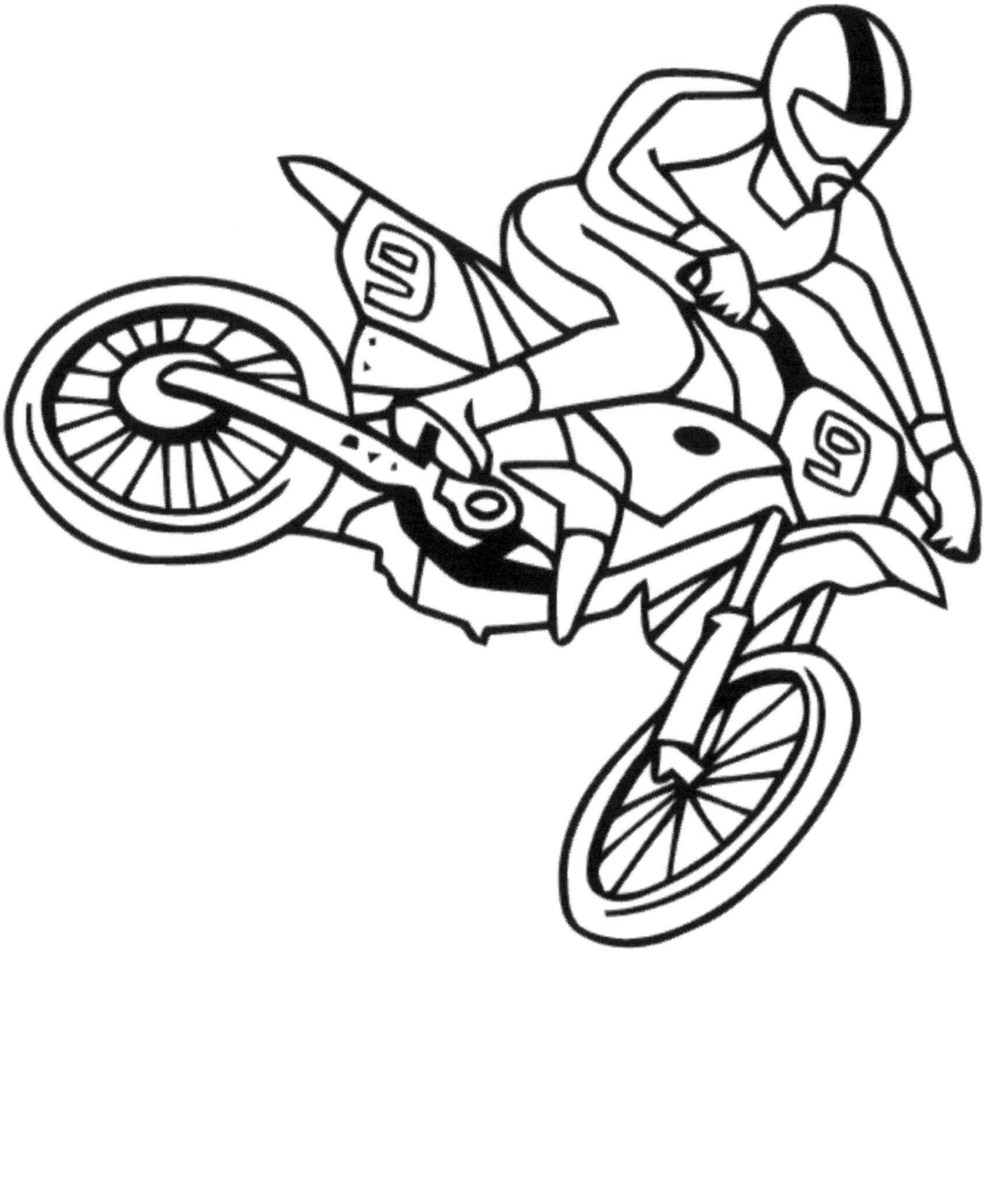

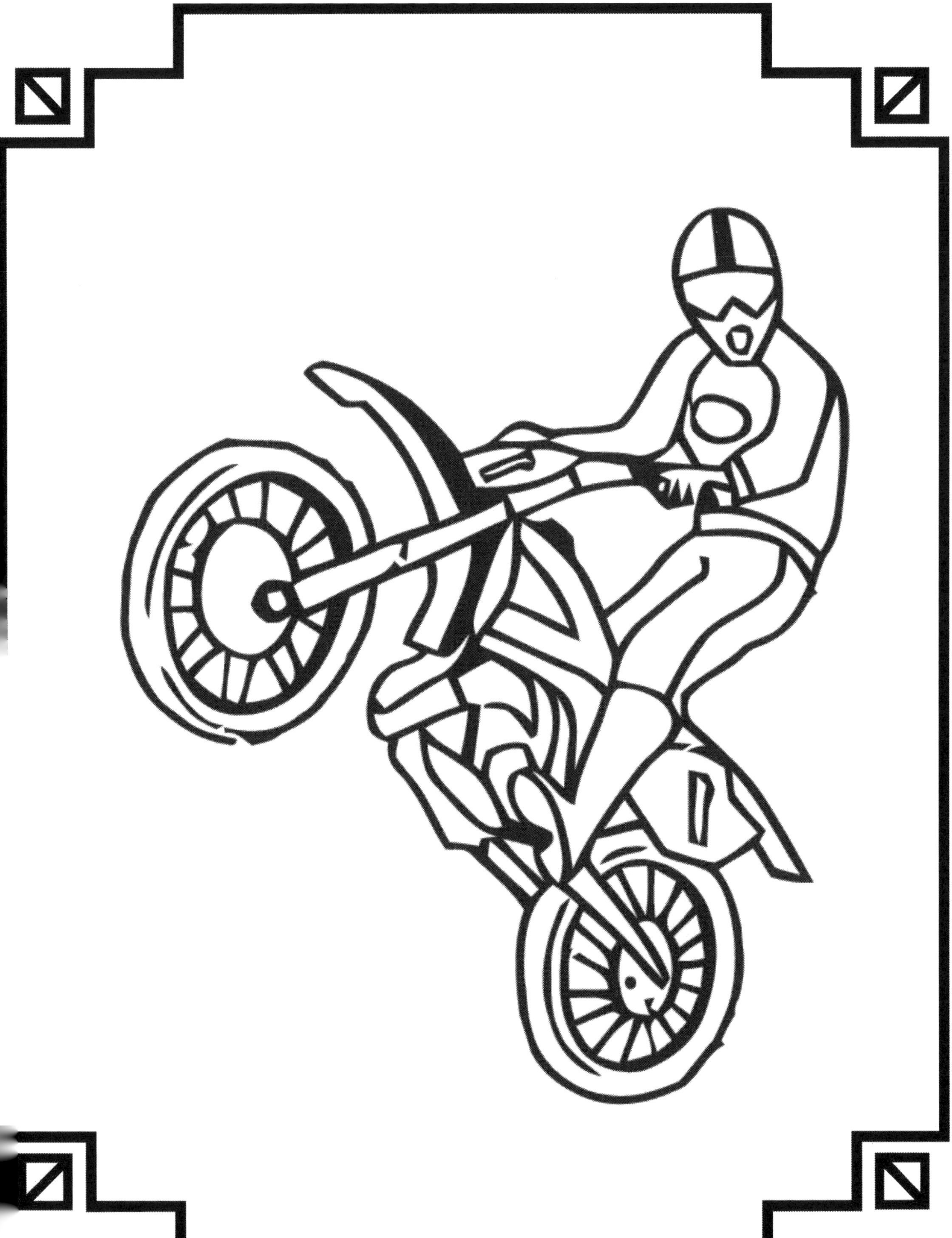

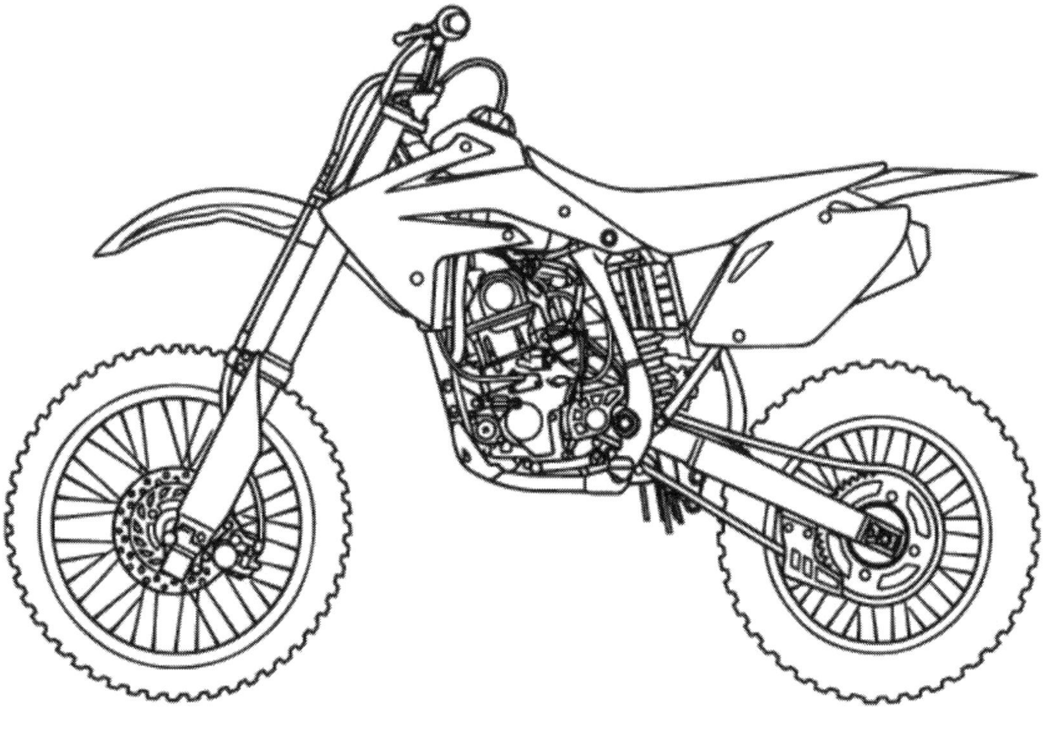

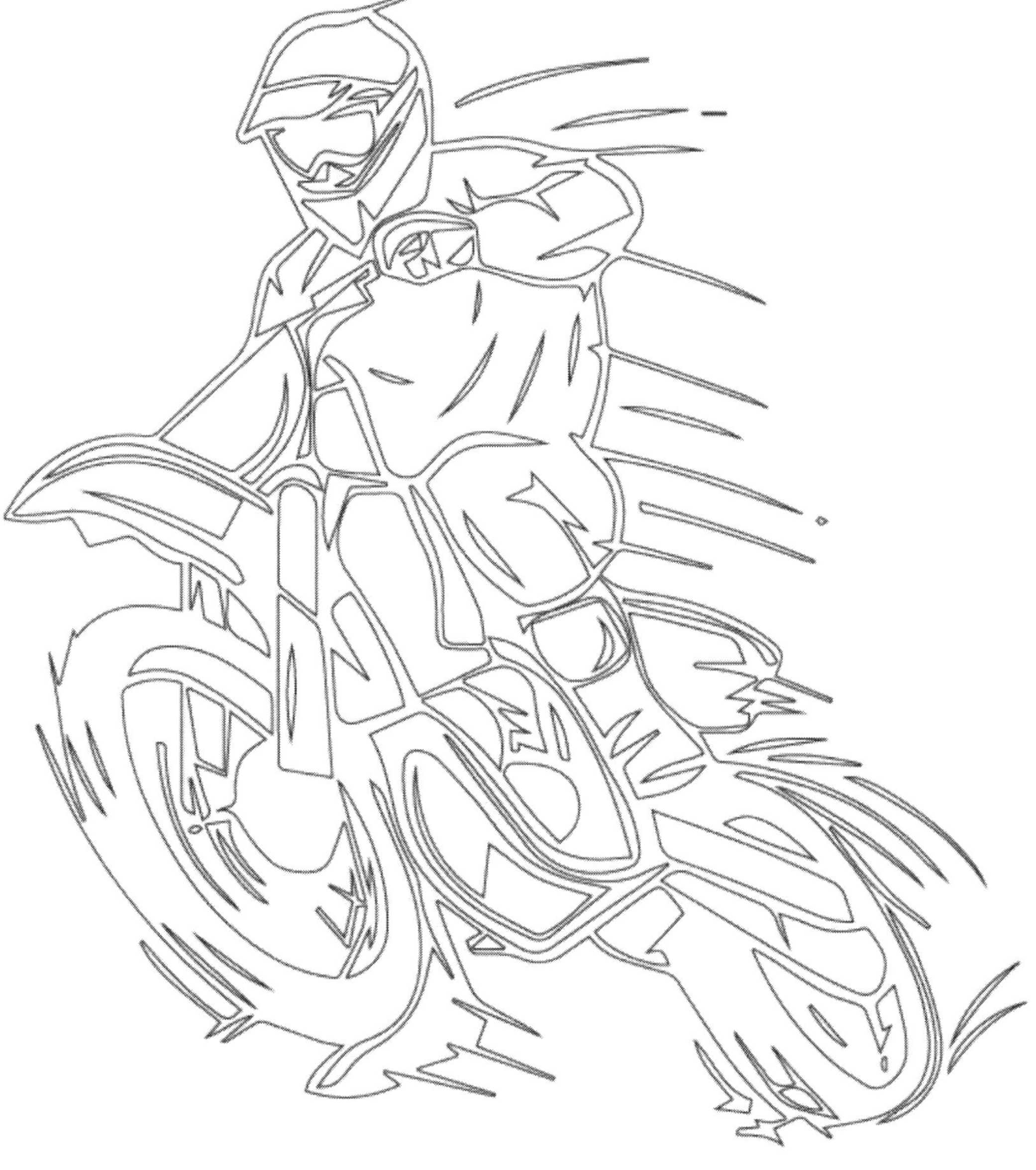

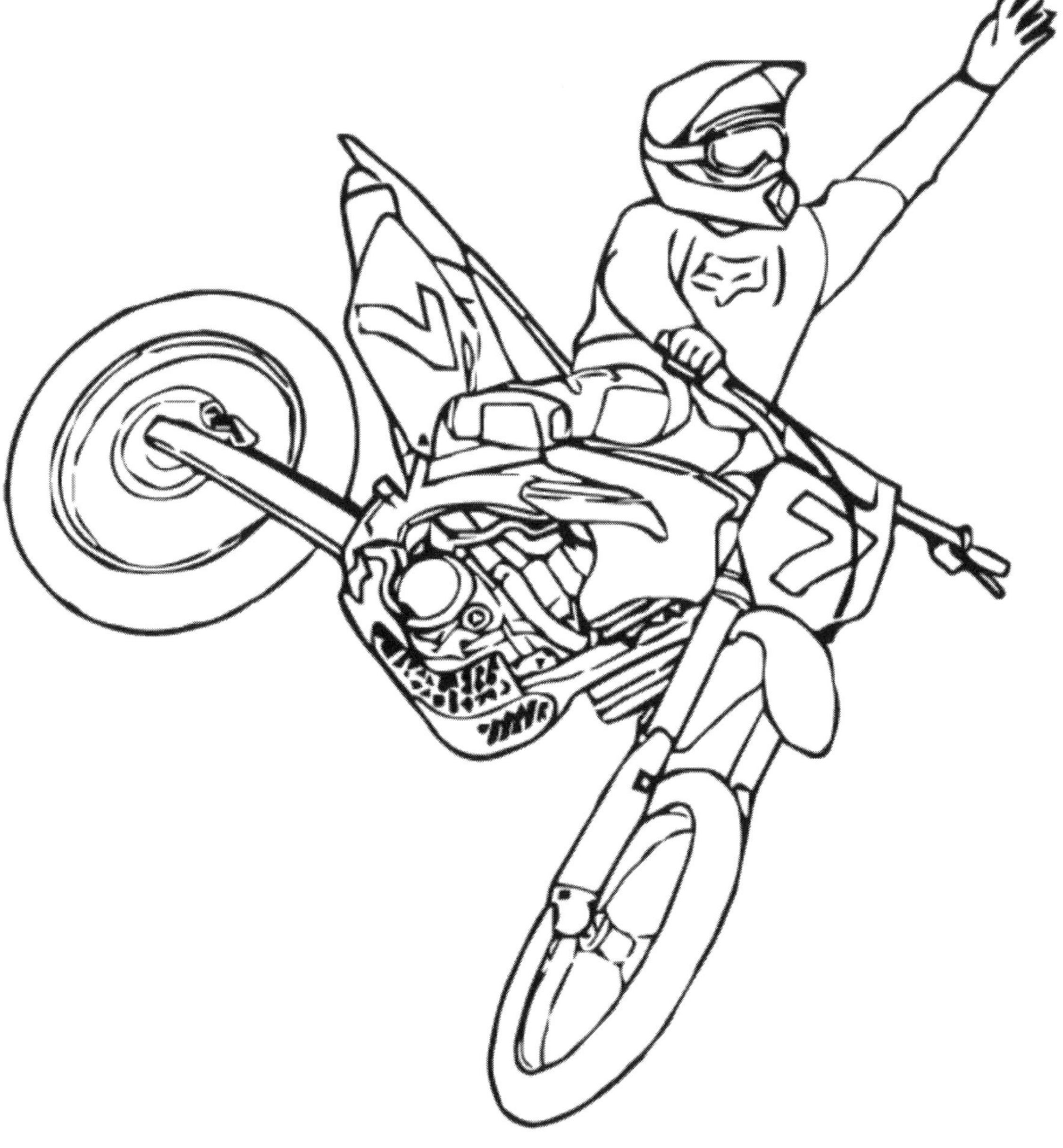

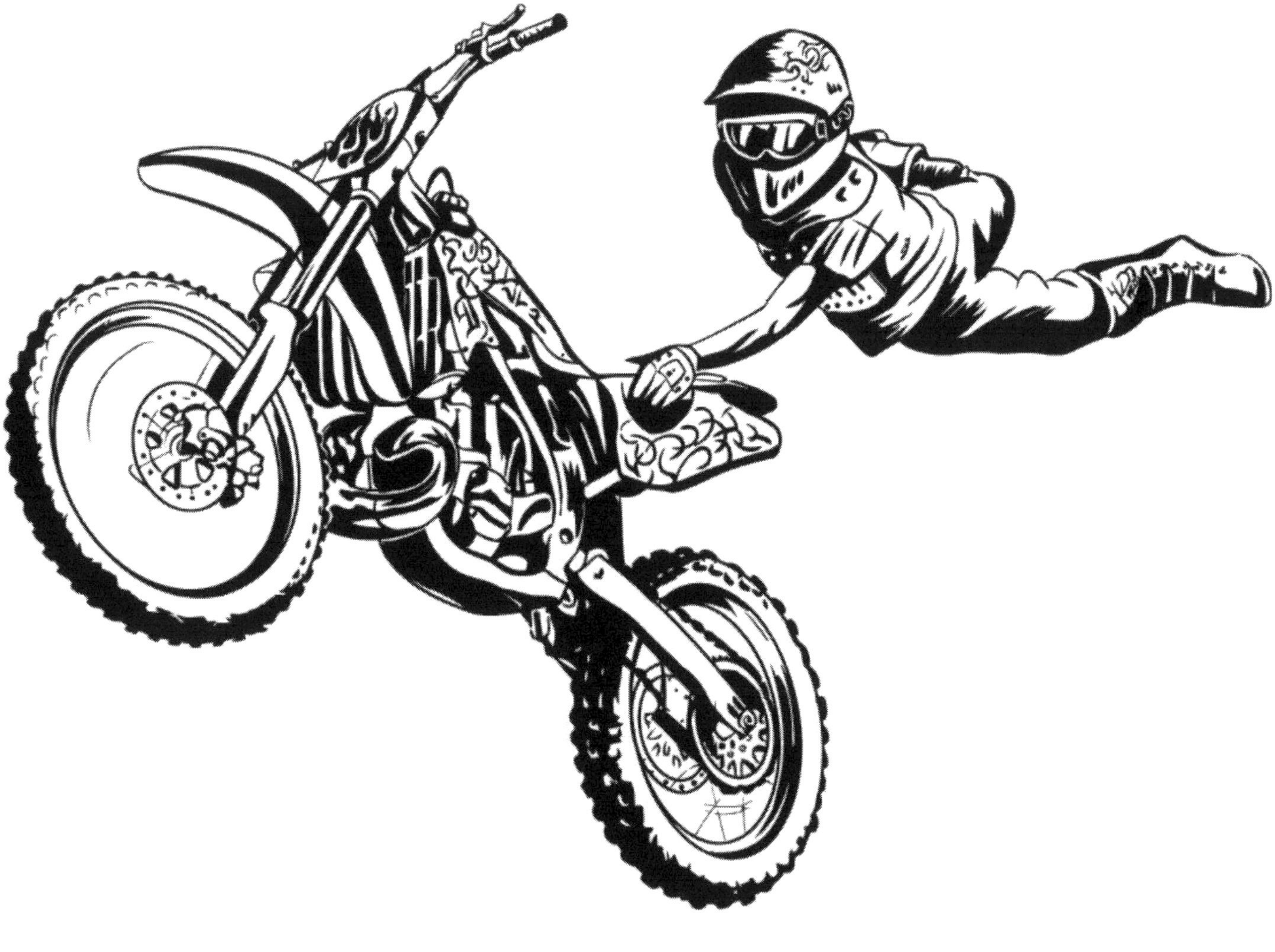

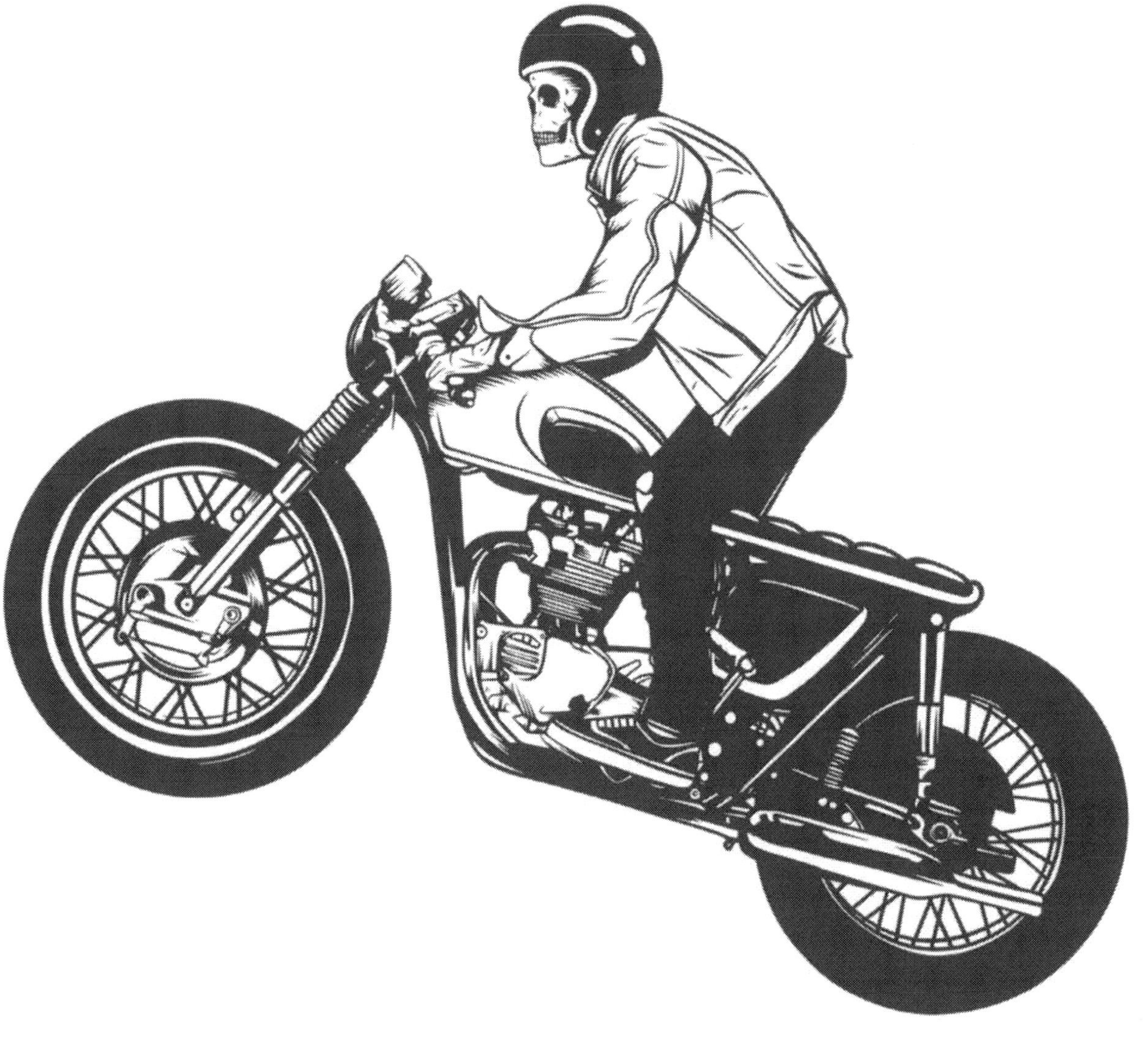

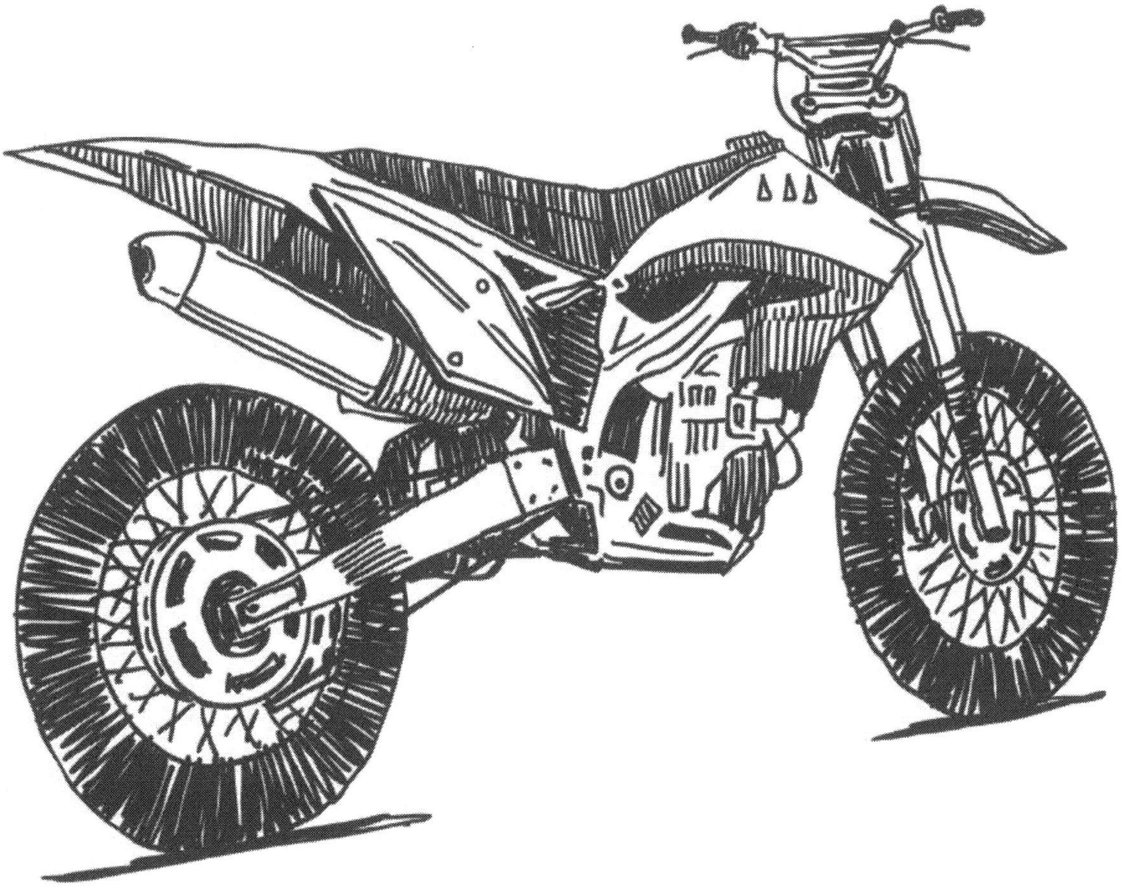

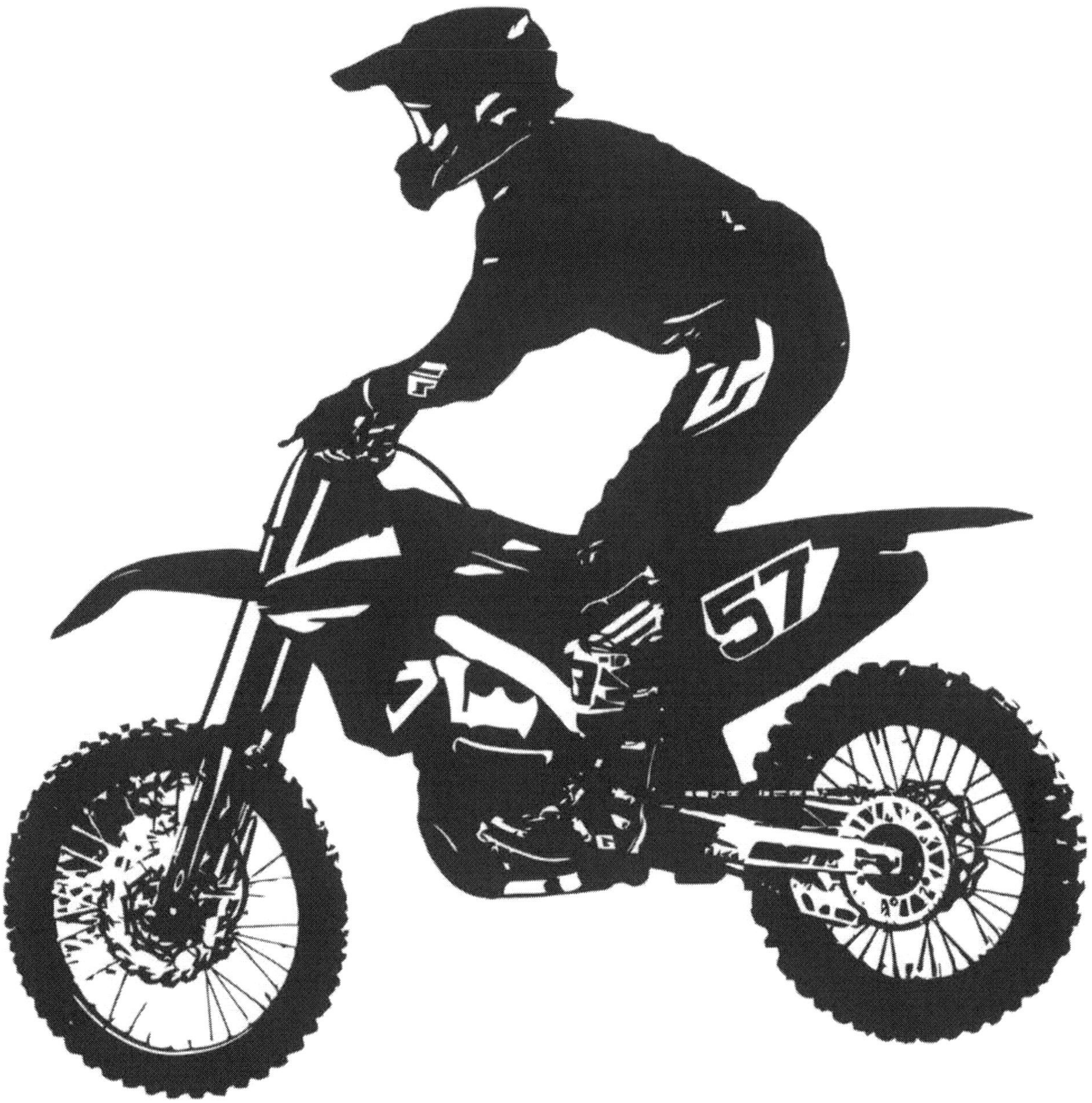
57

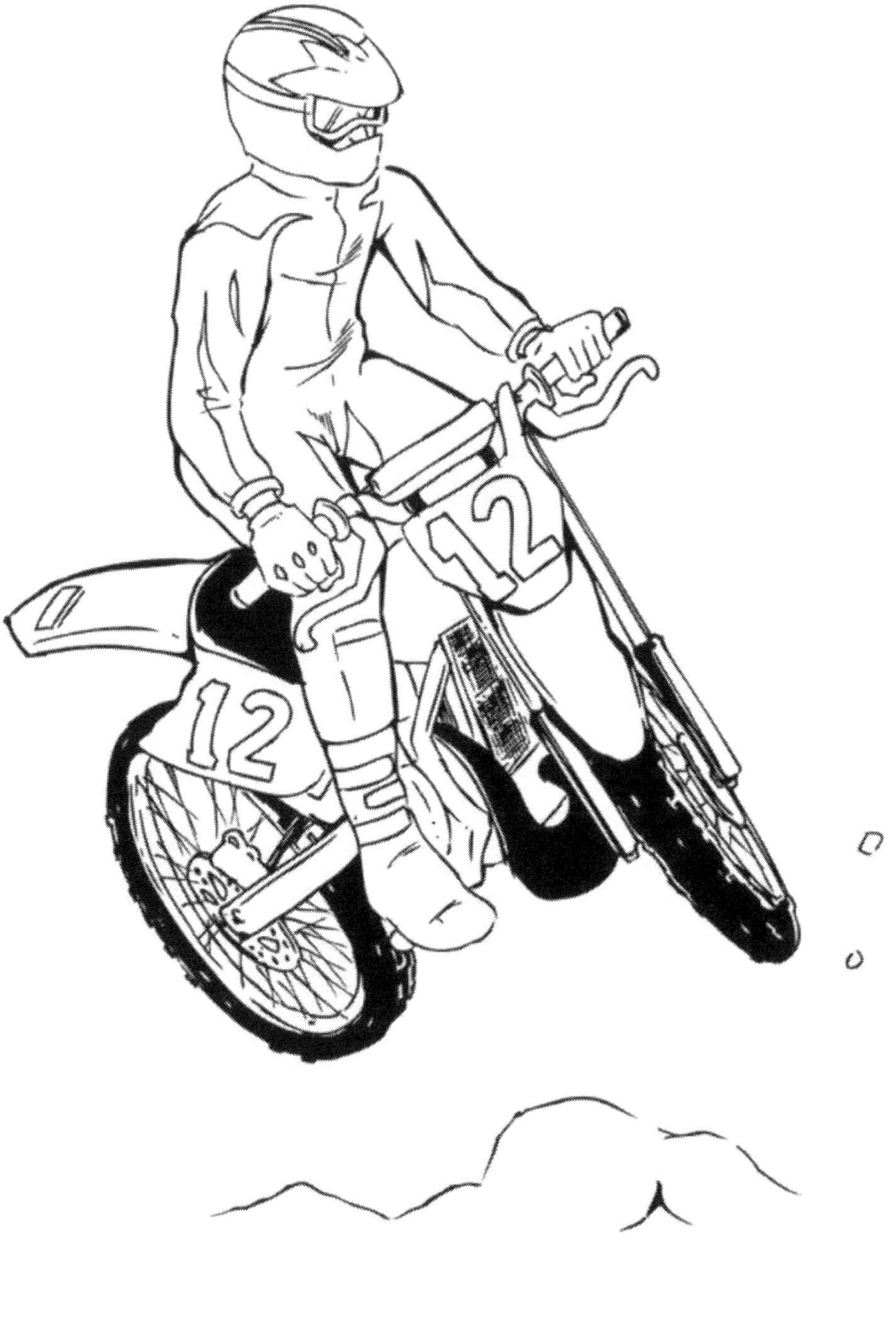
12
12

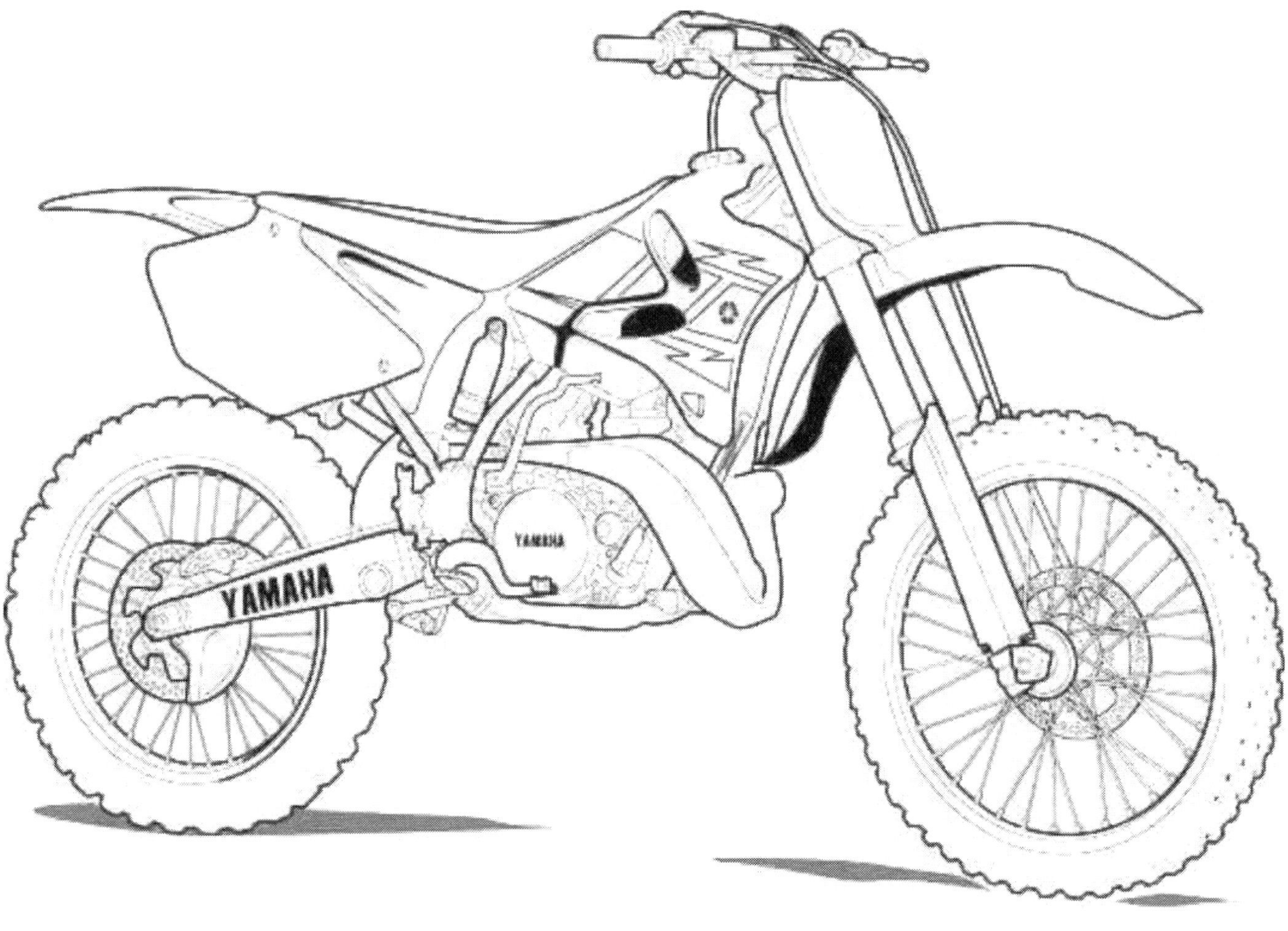
YAMAHA
YAMAHA

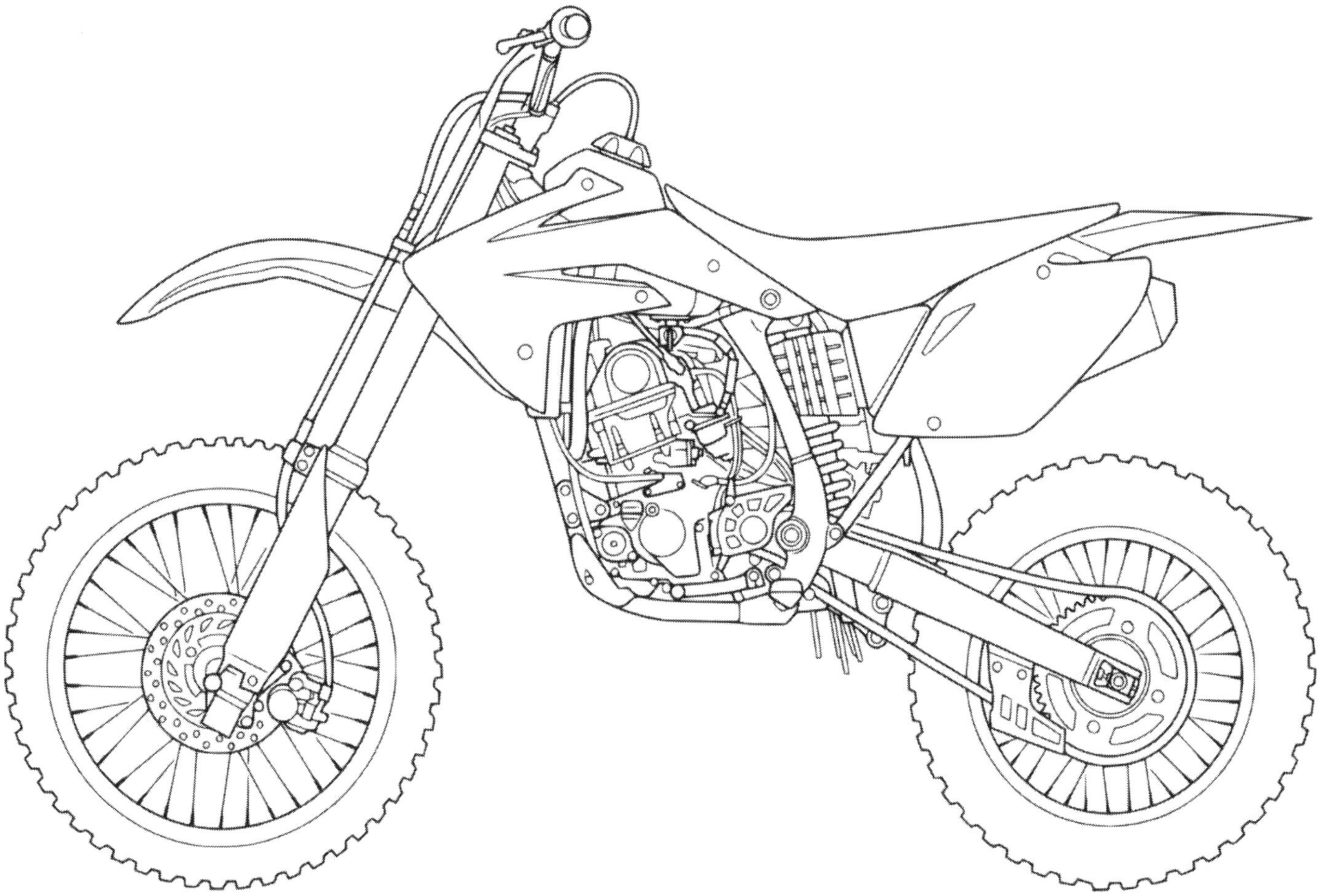

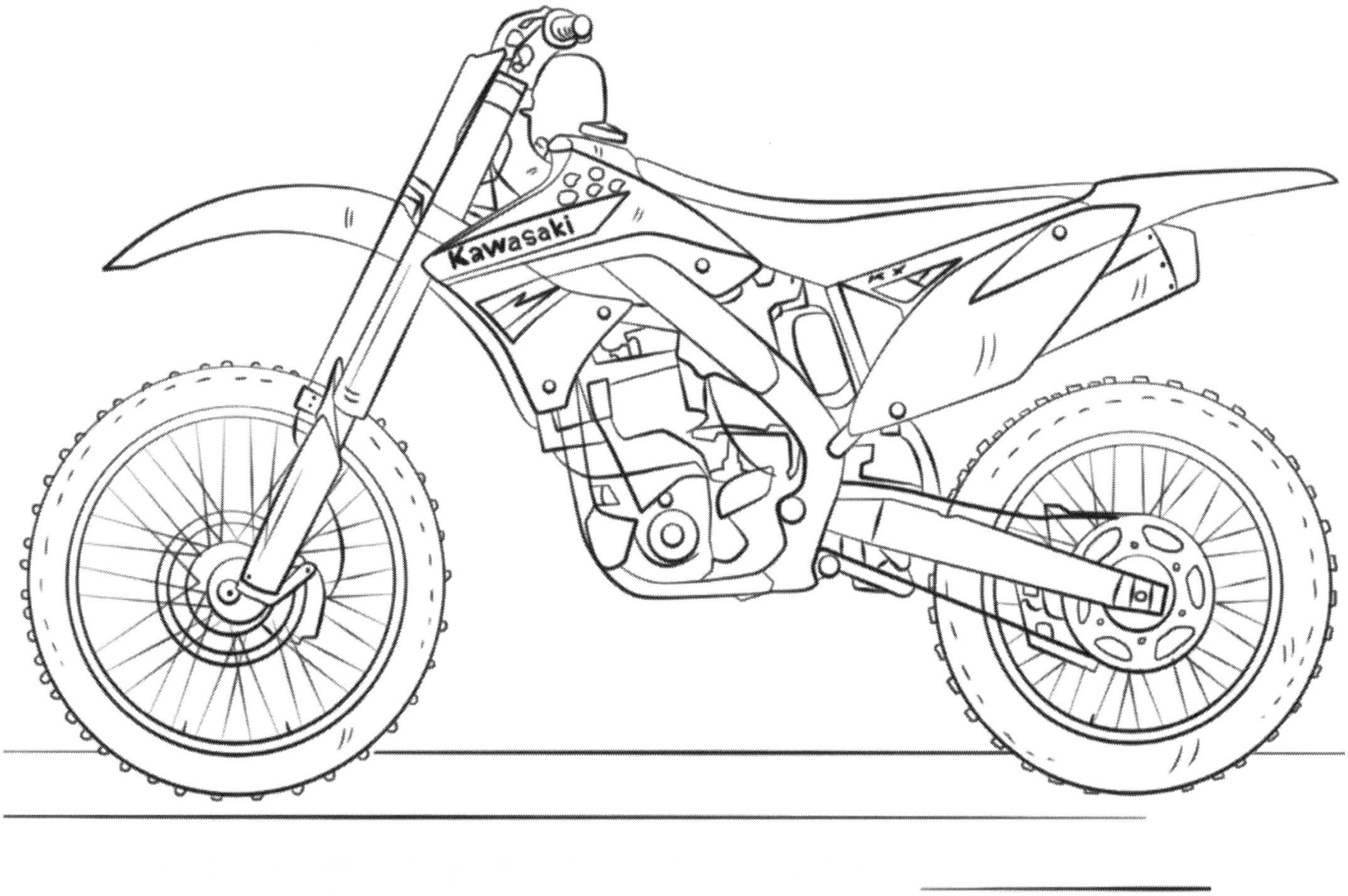
Kawasaki

Made in United States
Troutdale, OR
07/13/2023

11224220R00042